The Myth of
The
Chosen One

The Myth of
The
Chosen One

The Story Behind the Story
of the Man Who Allegedly Abused and Murdered
One Hundred Children

The Psychology of Serial Killers
Dr. K. Sohail

White Knight Publications
2002 Toronto, Canada

Published in 2002 by White Knight Publications,
A Division of Bill Belfontaine Ltd.
Suite 103, One Benvenuto Place, Toronto Ontario Canada M1N 1G2
E-mail: whitekn@istar.ca

Ordering information
Distributed in Canada by Hushion House Publishers Ltd.
c/o Georgetown Terminal Wharehouses, 34 Armstrong Avenue, Georgetown, ON, L7G 4R9
Phone (866) 485-5556, Fax (866) 485-6665, Email bsisnett@gtwcanada.com

National Library of Canada Cataloguing in Publication Data
Canadian Cataloguing in Publication Data
Sohail, K. (Khalid), 1952-
        The myth of the chosen one

ISBN 0-9730949-1-5

1. Mugal, Javed 2. Serial murderers—Psychology.
3. Infantcide

HV8079.H6S64 2001   364.15'23'092 C2001-902015-5

Editing:	Bill Belfontaine, Abbeyfield Consultants
	Toronto, Ontario
Cover / book design:	Karen Petherick, Intuitive Design International Ltd.,
	Peterborough, Ontario
Cover Photo:	Digital Imagery® 2002, Photodisk, Inc.
Printed/Bound in Canada:	TTP Tradeworx Ltd., Mississauga, Ontario

Dedication

Dedicated to those men and women
who were unjustly treated
by the justice system..

Table of Contents

Acknowledgements

Special thanks!

This book would not have been born if:

Zahid Lodhi, Saeed Anjum and Anne Aguirre had not supported me in my resolve to fly to Pakistan for this extraordinary experience.

Abid Hasan Minto had not helped me to obtain permission to interview Javed Iqbal Mughal and offered me his legal opinions on various aspects of the case.

Khawaja Shoaib, Irshad Mir, Zeeshan Mir, Shaukat Zain-ul-Abedin and Tausif Zain had not made it possible to visit Javed Iqbal Mughal's family and neighbours.

Dr. Tahir Mansoor had not offered his insights as a Rehabilitation specialist.

Anwar Ahmed had not provided free access to his private library.

Karen Petherick and Bill Belfontaine had not offered their creative suggestions.

and most of all,

Javed Iqbal Mughal had not shared his story in the death cell of a Lahore prison.

K. Sohail
Fall 2001

"The fact of this very human matter is that, as Willard Gaylin [American psychiatrist] has observed, 'In our unconscious we are all killers, rapists, incestual, exhibitionistic, voyeuristic, aggressive and homicidal.'

Many of us are programmed still further by our social system to displace our rage upon others: but why do individuals with equally tragic (or far more so) backgrounds chose not to kill? The fundamental act of humanity is to refuse to kill. Our murderers have consciously rejected that humanity. They are not robots programmed by some machine to do exactly what they do: they know precisely what they are doing.

For their betrayal of humanity, they deserve no better fate than to be permanently excised from the social order. Their only value is as objects of study."

Elliott Leyton, *Hunting Humans*
McClelland and Stewart Inc., Toronto, 1986.

"His mouth is full of curses and lies and threats; trouble and evil are under his tongue. He lies in wait near the villages; from ambush he murders the innocent, watching in secret for his victims. He lies in wait like a lion in cover, he lies in wait to catch the helpless, he catches the helpless and drags them off in his net. His victims are crushed, they collapse, they fall under his strength."

Psalms 10: 7-9

The case of *Javed Iqbal*, an alleged serial killer, attracted great attention both within and outside Pakistan. Killing of even one person is a heinous act, but here is a man attributed about a hundred cold-blooded murders of persons of young and tender ages. Allegations of child-abuse and the manner in which the dead bodies of the victims were destroyed and disposed of, compounded the gravity of the dastardly action. The man was tried along with his two young accomplices. The trial Court found enough evidence to convict all of them for the offences for which they were charged. The trial Judge while passing the sentence of death which by law he was entitled to award has further directed that the execution of sentence be done by publicly hanging the convict and that his dead body be cut into pieces and dissolved in acid. The Judge has no legal authority to do all that. Neither the statute law applicable to the case of Javed Iqbal nor any firmly established principle of Islamic law does furnish even a semblance of legality to the Judge's directions. It appears that the unusual part of Judge's directions is a reaction to the manner in which the convict is said to have disposed of the dead bodies.

Dr. Sohail has indeed taken pains to examine this shocking episode from the point of view of a Psychiatrist. We in Pakistan are not sufficiently equipped in that kind of investigation even at the clinical level. As for our investigating agencies, suffice it to say that their techniques and methods have not advanced during the last hundred years. Our Courts are not concerned with such matters, except when a plea of insanity is advanced on behalf of an accused person. So, Dr. Sohail's attempt is commendable. I wish, however, he had also had the opportunity to interview and in fact clinically examine the Judge who passed the order. It is not only the guilty who may be mentally sick, after all.

(Abid Hasan Minto)
Senior Advocate Supreme Court
Former *President* of the*Supreme Court Bar Association of Pakistan*

A Pakistani Serial Killer and The Judge

March 17, 2000 Canada

It started as an ordinary but ended as a very extra-ordinary day for me.

After saying goodbye to the last of my patients at my psychotherapy clinic, and to my colleague Anne Aguirre, I went home anticipating a quiet evening. During dinner while watching the Canadian news on television, I was quite surprised to find Pakistan as the subject of a major news story. The reporter stated that Javed Iqbal Mughal, a resident of Lahore, had been convicted of abusing and killing one hundred children. Judge Allah Bakhash Ranjha, had pronounced the verdict that not only should he be publicly hanged, but also that his dead body should be cut into a hundred pieces and dissolved in a drum of acid.

The newscast was accompanied by pictures of Javed Iqbal and the judge. I found the news so disturbing that I could not finish my dinner. There was something very unusual about the images of the criminal and the judge. The more I thought about them, the more I realized that Javed Iqbal looked very calm, peaceful and relaxed while the judge seemed very angry, resentful and revengeful. The criminal did not seem as disturbed, nor the judge as well composed and sober, as I would have expected. There was something about Javed Iqbal's features, his looks and his posture that touched me deeply. He had not uttered a word on the screen but his silence spoke volumes. I had an intuition that there was a story behind the story on the news.

That night when I went to bed, I tried to get rid of those images from my mind but I could not. And then I heard a whisper in my heart, "You are a psychiatrist. You should go and interview him in his death cell. Maybe he did not kill one hundred children. Maybe he is the black sheep who has become the scapegoat of the corrupt system. He does not look like a criminal."

I tried to ignore the whisper. But the more I tried to silence it, the louder it got. I had never been affected so intensely by any news in all my life. The next day when I discussed the story with a couple of friends and expressed a desire to go to Pakistan to interview Javed Iqbal, they thought I was out of my mind.

The next night when I went to bed I heard another whisper that said, "Maybe Javed Iqbal suffers from mental illness. Maybe he should be in a mental asylum rather than a death cell." I was not sure whether in Pakistan there was a tradition of the judge ordering a psychiatric consultation prior to sentencing for people accused of serious crimes.

The next morning I called my friend Zahid Ali who has a number of connections with lawyers and politicians and asked him if he could get me a copy of the judge's verdict. In a couple of days it came delivered by Zahid. It was the most disturbing document that I had come across in my entire career. It confirmed my suspicion that the judge had not requested a psychiatric consultation and that he was very angry and punitive. He had written in his judgement:

> "He is a Satan in the shape of a human being. In fact he is a beast and such a cruel man that it is a disgrace to humanity to label him as human....The prosecution has fully succeeded in proving and with the Grace of God I am fully convinced that the accused have committed the Qatal Amad [first degree murder] of 100 children and after cutting their dead bodies into pieces have put the dead bodies into drums recovered from the house of Javed Iqbal accused. He should be strangulated with an iron chain, the weapon of offence in this case, in the presence of legal heirs of the deceased and then his dead body should be cut into pieces as it has been proved that he used to cut the dead bodies of the children deceased in this case. The pieces of his dead body should be put into a drum containing the formula modus operandi used by the accused for dissolving the dead body ... the sentence be executed at an open place, preferably Minar-e-Pakistan, (historical monument in a large park) in the presence of the legal heirs of the deceased children in order to make it a horrible example."

Dr. K. Sohail

As I read the verdict, my mind suddenly filled with questions.

- Why, out of thousands of people who go through the criminal system, had the judge chosen Javed Iqbal to be "a horrible example"?
- Did the judge overstep his authority and order an execution that was illegal?
- What was Javed Iqbal's reaction to the punishment?

After studying the verdict, my urge to fly to Pakistan grew very strong. But to do that I had to close my clinic for a few days. When I shared my idea with my colleague and nurse, Anne Aguirre, she pondered the idea for some time before answering. She has worked in Central America, and traveled extensively, so she is aware of the unpredictable shifts in political winds. She also looks after the clinic billings and I could see her mentally calculating the cost-benefit ratio of my proposed trip. "If the army is in power and Javed Iqbal is in prison awaiting execution, what do you think your chances are of being able to interview him?" she asked.

"In Pakistan, every impossible thing can be made possible," I replied.

"How so?"

"By knowing the right people."

Anne remained dubious, then said, "The problem is that the permission you get from one person can be rescinded by somebody else, and you would never know why."

However, I am an adventurous person and I was prepared to take the risk for what I felt was an unprecedented learning opportunity.

I thought of all the people I knew who could help me in this project. The desire to go to Pakistan was quickly transformed into a plan. I felt driven by it. Finally I thought of Mr. Abid Hasan Minto, a well-respected Supreme Court lawyer who resided in Lahore. I had met him in Sweden during an International conference of Asian writers a few years before; I had presented a paper and he had presided over some of the meetings in the conference. Afterward we had met socially. He was very kind and affectionate. I called my friend Saeed Anjum in

Norway, who had introduced me to Mr. Minto. Saeed Anjum not only gave me Mr. Minto's phone number but also offered me a lot of moral support. He encouraged me to continue with my plan.

I was pleasantly surprised that Mr. Minto picked up the phone himself. After the initial formalities, I asked him if he could help me in arranging an interview with Javed Iqbal Mughal. He said he would try his best to get me the necessary permission and asked me to give him a couple of days to make some calls. When I talked to him next, he told me that he had spoken to one of the ministers in the Secretariat who had promised to help me. He also suggested that I fly to Pakistan right away because nobody knew when Javed Iqbal might be publicly hanged. I was becoming increasingly concerned because we had very little time to waste.

Anne cancelled my appointments for a week and I called my travel agent to book the first flight to Pakistan. To get an early flight I had to pay $1700 rather than the regular $1200. My passion was worth the sacrifice of $500.

When I called my family and my cousin, Khawaja Shoaib, they were thrilled to hear the news of my upcoming visit to Pakistan. Shoaib had always been very helpful whenever I visited Lahore and, in return, I was always impressed by his generosity of spirit. When I shared with him the nature of my visit he reassured me that he would take a few days off work to help me with my most unusual project.

◫ 2 *When Murderers Are Mentally Ill*

While preparing for my mysterious journey to Pakistan, I reminisced about my twenty years in Canada as a practising psychiatrist. Since I had a keen interest in personality problems, I had over the years worked with a large number of people who were diagnosed as delinquents, sociopaths and psychopaths. Many of them had been in trouble with the law and had served time in jail. There was a time when I was assigned to the Forensic unit and had to do psychiatric assessments for the court. I remembered a few visits to the jail to assess people for the

Crown. For a number of years I attended meetings of the Ontario Review Board to fight for the rights of patients who had committed serious crimes but who suffered from serious mental illness. I had always advocated a compassionate rather than a punitive approach and I believed in rehabilitation rather than incarceration. My recommendations were always for a therapeutic environment even in the sometime brutal, always revengeful, prison system.

Of all the people I had served in the last two decades, there were two patients who had left strong impressions in my mind. Their stories were hard to forget. Both patients suffered from Paranoid Schizophrenia and had spent years in the psychiatric hospital system because they had committed murders. The first one had killed his wife while psychotic. He believed that his wife had had an affair with his friend. After years of treatment his illness was under control. Each year he promised the Review Board that he would comply with the treatment plan voluntarily but the Review Board would not set him free. He used to see me every week and complained about the controlling system we lived in, the dark ages of mental health care.

Finally he disappeared. Neither the hospital staff nor the police could find him. Years passed and we heard nothing about him.

Then one day I got a call from the police that they were bringing him from the airport to be readmitted. When I met him he was quite rational and stable. He had been living in Winnipeg, working regularly and responsibly as an electrician and residing peacefully in a two-bedroom apartment. Nobody would have found him had there not been a murder in the building where he lived. When the police were investigating the murder, they found out that he had walked away from the supervision of a psychiatric hospital in Ontario. He was arrested and sent back. I tried to fight his case, stating that during his stay out of the province he had not broken any law and he was no threat to society. But my arguments were not convincing enough for the administrators and he was re-admitted to the hospital. His story had inspired me to write my novel, *A Broken Man*.

The second patient was a man in his fifties. He had a tracheotomy, which made it difficult for him to talk. While in a psychotic state, he had killed his mother. The interesting thing was that since he was found not guilty by reason of insanity, he had inherited half a million dollars after his mother's death. Some cynics felt he was being rewarded for killing his mother. The other interesting aspect of his story was that when he had his first psychotic episode as a teenager he had told his doctor that he suffered from throat cancer, but the doctor told him that it was his delusion. But at the age of fifty, he was diagnosed with cancer of the throat and required a tracheotomy. He told the doctor, "I have been telling you people for the last thirty years that I have cancer of the throat, but nobody believed me." The doctor had no answer.

Thinking of Javed Iqbal, I was sure that if he lived in Canada, he would have been seen by a psychiatrist for an assessment.

Anne was supportive of my passion, but still concerned that Javed Iqbal might refuse to talk to me, or that his lawyer might have advised him not to give any interviews. But I was optimistic that I would be successful in interviewing him. It was just my intuition, but I wanted to follow it and think positively, and keep my journey from becoming a crusade against what I perceived to be a grave injustice.

⊠ 3 *America: World's Highest Rate of Serial Killers and Mass Murderers*

If we explore the subject of multiple murderers before reaching Iqbal, we discover the fascinating statistic that the incidence of serial killers and mass murderers has been gradually increasing worldwide in the last few decades. It is further intriguing to find that America has the highest rate of killings per capita.

Steve Egger in his collection of essays, *Serial Murder*, states that "America produces proportionately more of these killers than any other nation on earth." Elliott Leyton in his book *Hunting Humans* (McClelland & Stewart Inc., Toronto, 1986) writes, "... their numbers do continue to grow at a disturbing rate; until the 1960s they were anomalies who appeared perhaps once a decade, but by the 1980s, one was spawned virtually each month. Today, according to unofficial U.S. Justice Department estimates, there may be as many as one hundred multiple murderers killing in America, stealing the lives of thousands."

Why such a shocking increase lately and why primarily in America? This question has commanded the attention of many psychologists, sociologists and anthropologists and remains an ongoing study.

Some blame it on the industrial revolution. They believe that as people move from rural to urban residences, they leave their extended families behind and get lost in metropolitan cities. Loss of social support networks creates a state of isolation and alienation, which play a major part in aggressive outbursts.

Others blame it on economic and social injustices. They believe that in capitalistic stratified societies there is a large gap between rich and poor. There are millions in the United States living below the poverty line, deprived of decent housing, health insurance, social support agencies and other necessities.

Stuart Palmer writes, "The poor, the uneducated, those without legitimate opportunities, respond to their institutionalized oppression with outward explosions of aggression."

It is not uncommon to see that people who are chronically frustrated gradually become more and more angry and then, at a certain breaking point, that anger is transformed into aggression and violence. Quite often such violence is directed towards those people and institutions that are perceived as oppressive. At times it becomes very generalized and such murderers start killing indiscriminately, always driven by the same self-limitations.

Some experts consider racial inequalities and unjust treatment of minorities to be a significant factor in understanding violence in the community. Kirk Williams' tentative conclusion in the sociological journals remains that ... "racial ... economic inequality is a major source of criminal violence in the United States," and that "poverty, in addition to racial inequality, also provides fertile soil for criminal violence."

And then there are others who consider emotional insecurity more important than financial insecurity. They feel that only those who become morally and spiritually bankrupt with no hope of regaining their self-worth pick up guns to kill others.

Williams continues, "He [Phillip Lindsay in *Mainspring of Murder*] also noted the strange paradox that it did not seem to be economic insecurity (which had always been with us) but personal and spiritual insecurity that formed the breeding ground for the modern multiple murderer." *Ref. 1 - Hunting Humans, Elliot Leyton, McClelland & Stewart /Toronto 1986* It is interesting to see that the loss of meaning and purpose in life is related to the rise not only of murders but also of suicide in the twentieth century.

There are still others who believe that the concept of the American Dream plays a major role in these catastrophic tragedies. When people are encouraged to believe that they can dream big, and that anything and everything is possible, then when such a dream is shattered, the disappointment leads to bitterness and thoughts of revenge or self-destruction.

It is fascinating to observe the evolution of American society in the twentieth century. One can see the best and the worst of the whole world in the United States of America. People from everywhere are trying to emigrate to America, as though it were the modern "promised land". In this land of eminent scientists, avant-garde artists and Oscar award-winning actors and directors, we also see the worst serial killers and mass murderers. It seems that America has become the world of extremes.

◼ 4 *A Profile of Modern Serial Killers and Mass Murderers*

Over the years, I have been preoccupied with the questions:

Who are the people who choose to become serial killers and
    mass murderers?
What kind of families do they come from?
What kind of childhood do they have?
What kind of personalities do they develop?

Dr. K. Sohail

While reviewing literature and studying the personalities and lifestyles of modern serial killers and mass murderers I became aware that they are different than:

1. Murderers who get involved in tribal warfare and kill members of rival tribes.
2. One-time murderers who kill their enemy in the heat of passion. These murderers know their enemy intimately.
3. Murderers who kill people for profit as they have chosen the profession of becoming a criminal hit man.
4. Those murderers who are members of a political party or government, and who kill their enemies in a very systematic way. In the twentieth century, thousands of people have been killed by members of left wing communist parties and right wing fundamentalists in various parts of the world.

The hallmark of modern serial killers and mass murderers is that they kill innocent strangers. The psychiatrist Lunde has made it clear that "the most important single contrast between mass murderers and murderers of a single person is their relationship to the victims, the former killing strangers, the latter killing intimates." *(Ref. 1 p. 261)*

While studying the biographies of serial killers and mass murderers, when I focused on their families, I discovered that they belong to two distinct groups.

The first group consists of those individuals who are either adopted, grew up in institutions or were brought up by abusive parents. They never receive loving and nurturing care from their parents in a consistent manner. They are exposed to severe neglect and different forms of abuse and have poor role models. They grow up to be angry and bitter individuals.

Henry Lee Lucas, from Texas, who confessed to killing more than 300 people, described the family environment of his childhood, "That's the way I grew up when I was a child — watching my mom have sexual acts. She wouldn't go into different rooms, she'd make sure I was in the room before she started anything, and she would do it deliberately to make me watch her, you know, I got so I hated it." *(Ref. 1 p. 23)*

While Lucas was wrongly treated by his mother, Michael Wayne McGray, the Canadian serial killer, and Albert De Salvo, the Boston Strangler, were abused by their fathers. De Salvo's father used to beat his wife and son regularly. Albert witnessed his father breaking bones of his mother's fingers one by one. McGray's father, who was a violent alcoholic, used to beat animals regularly and encouraged his son to do the same. Peter Kurten, a German serial killer also had a troubled childhood. His father when drunk used to force his wife to have sex in front of their children. Their fathers were angry and cruel men.

Many abused children who grow up to become serial killers and mass murderers in turn abuse animals even as children. Many of them learn it from their parents. Peter Kurten's father taught him how to masturbate and torture dogs as a child. Cruelty to animals seems a significant sign for later development of psychopathic personality and murderous lifestyle.

The second group consists of serial killers and mass murderers who grow up in loving and caring families and are usually spoiled or over-indulged. They are generally successful in school and grow up with high ideals and dreams. But if as young adults their dreams are shattered because of socio-economic injustices and prejudices, they can transform into angry, resentful and revengeful people.

Mark Essex, an American, was raised in a middle class family, nurtured and loved by his parents. He wanted to become a minister. During a stint in the Navy, he faced a lot of prejudice and discrimination and was called a Nigger. When he finally turned against white people, he killed nine and injured ten more by setting a hotel fire.

Lay people might consider most modern serial killers and mass murderers "mad", but in the view of mental health professionals, they do not show signs and symptoms of mental illness. Instead, they suffer from Psychopathic Personality Disorder.

Thinking back to the literature I had read over the years, I wondered whether Javed Iqbal had more similarities or differences with other serial killers of the world.

Dr. K. Sohail

5 A Journey: Pakistan and the Unknown

During my 26-hour flight on PIA (Pakistan International Airlines) from Toronto to Lahore, I reminisced about my life in Pakistan and my reasons for leaving my troubled motherland. I had always felt suffocated in that restrictive environment. My creative writing and my non-traditional lifestyle and philosophy were always perceived as a threat to my family and community. The last straw was when I was at medical school and Zulfiqar Ali Bhutto's government had declared Ahmedis followers of Mirza Ghulam Ahmed, non-muslims. Although I was not an Ahmedi myself, I had sympathies for the minorities. I believed that all citizens of the country should have equal rights and privileges. I was afraid that with my attitude, if I had stayed in Pakistan, I might have found myself in jail or in a mental hospital.

In spite of my struggles in my motherland, I still had fond memories of Lahore, the capital city I was visiting. Although I spent most of my life in the city of Peshawar, I always looked forward to my visits to Lahore. As a child I loved visiting my grandmother from whom I inherited my humanistic values, and as a teenager I would visit my poet uncle, Arif Abdul Mateen, who was a fountain of wisdom and creativity. As a young adult, when I began writing poems and short stories, I would go to the Pak Tea House where all of the well-known poets and writers and intellectuals got together every evening. They were a source of inspiration for me.

I perceived Lahore as a city of saints and scholars. Millions of people from all over the world come to see the cultural, literary and artistic events in Lahore. Tourists get the impression that there are eight festivals in seven days in that city, the city that is the heart of Punjab and Pakistan. Highlights of a visit to Lahore include the holy shrine of Ali Hajveri who is known by his disciples as Data Ganj Baksh (the one who offers treasures). His book *Kashful-mehjoob* (Revelation of Secrets) has become an important part of mystic literature. There is the annual *Charaghon ka maila* (Festival of Lights) in the memory of a saint Madhu Lal Hussain in the Shalamar Gardens, the Minar-e-Pakistan, which one might call the CN Tower of Pakistan, the Lahore Fort, the tomb of the famous poet Mohammad Iqbal and the Badshahi Mosque, the biggest in the world, where 50,000 people can pray at the same time. It is interesting and amusing that the *Heera Mandi* (Red Light Area) is next to the mosque. It seems as though the saints and the sinners walk next to each other in those streets.

This time I was not going primarily to see my family or meet my writer friends and artists but to interview Javaid Iqbal to determine the following:

Does he suffer from a mental illness?
Is he a psychopath?
What kind of upbringing did he have?
Did he question the social taboos and challenge the sacred
    traditions of his community?

Many more things that I could not freely articulate to myself came to mind. I was in a new territory feeling apprehensive yet excited at the same time. It was becoming a journey into the unknown ... .

⧗ 6   *In the Eyes of the Law*

After spending some time with my family and resting to recover from jet lag, I called Mr. Minto's home. His son told me that he was out of town to attend a political meeting and would be back the next day. When I called back, Mr. Minto asked, "Why don't you come to my office tomorrow and we can go to the Secretariat together." I quickly agreed.

The next day the minister received us respectfully and asked other visitors in the waiting room to be patient till he was free. After the introductions, the minister called the Inspector General of Prisons. He turned on the speaker part of the telephone so that we could hear his conversation. "Dr. Sohail is here. He is a psychiatrist and is doing research on serial killers. He would like to interview Javed Iqbal."

The voice in reply was hollow. "That is not possible, Sir. He is in his death cell under maximum security. We cannot let anybody see him. He will be hanged any day."

There was a long discomforting pause. Then the minister said, "Dr. Sohail has brought Mr. Abid Hasan Minto, my respected teacher with him. I just cannot say no to him."

"If that is the case, Sir, then send Dr. Sohail with a letter and I will make sure he interviews Javed Iqbal."

"Thank you very much. I really appreciate your cooperation."

The minister dictated the letter right away. We said goodbye and left.

While we were driving back I asked Mr. Minto, "Does the Pakistani Penal Code allow capital punishment?"

He thought for a few seconds and then said, "Well, as far as Pakistani penal law is concerned, it continues to have capital punishment on various accounts. Mostly on account of all those cases where death is caused in the consequence of a criminal act, the punishment is always death. That is right from the days of Anglo-Saxon laws and right from the days of the British. That is the penal code of Pakistan. It is the same law as in India. This same law prevails in all the countries of the Dominion and the colonies of the British. After Independence, there have been some additions to the laws of Pakistan in which capital punishment is now being awarded. They are called "Hadood Laws", which are the Islamic version of some penal laws. In some of those laws capital punishment is provided.

"Similarly there is an addition of the Hijacking Law under which if there is a hijacking committed and some deaths occur as a consequence then that punishment is also awarded. So there is capital punishment as a rule available in the penal law of Pakistan in cases which are considered to be too heinous and too serious."

When we reached his home he invited me in for refreshment, and we entered his tastefully-decorated living room. His wife, a well-known short story writer, served us tea and snacks. I wanted to take full advantage of the opportunity at hand using Mr. Minto's experience, so I asked him, "In the case of Javed Iqbal, alongside capital punishment, the judge has also ordered public hanging. Has there been any previous case of public hanging in the history of Pakistan?"

Sipping tea first, Mr. Minto replied, "Yes, in the history of Pakistan, there has been one case of public hanging and that was during the martial law of Zia-ul-Haq. And the martial law of Zia-ul-Haq was a typical martial law in the sense that it introduced into the permanent law of Pakistan several provisions, which created a deviation from the settled norms of the law. He also introduced whipping and some other punishments, which according to his version were Islamic punishments.

"He ordered public hanging of three persons who were convicted of the offence of murder of a young child. That was done publicly but after that, no more public hanging has taken place. Quite a few months back there was an order by a certain court for a public hanging of an accused person but that was opposed by all the conscientious people in Pakistan. Liberal politicians and even some liberal Islamics raised their voice against the public hanging and ultimately the matter was taken up by the Supreme Court of Pakistan in its recent jurisdiction and then there was no public hanging. So there has not been a public hanging since that event which took place during the previous martial law of Zia-ul-Haq."

I pushed the issue further by asking, "In the case of Javed Iqbal, the judge, alongside public hanging had also ordered that the dead body be cut into a hundred pieces and put in acid drum the way Javed Iqbal dealt with the victims. What do you think of that?"

"Yes, this is very interesting," he said. "You see there are situations in which even the judicial officers are caught up in the events and the general sentiments of the people. Perhaps the judge was taken over by the general demand of exemplary punishment of the accused. And he thought exemplary punishment could only be a punishment equal to the type of torture that he had been perpetuating on his victims. So he ordered something which is not permitted by the law; saying that the dead body has to be cut into a hundred pieces and dissolved in acid and then thrown away is not provided for by the law. It was the imagination of the judge that was working there. His judgements was overwhelmingly criticized in the newspapers.

"According to the law you can give sentence or punishment to a person who is alive. Punishment is to a human being. Punishment cannot be to a dead body so the sentence he pronounced on a dead body cannot be justified.

14   D r .   K .   S o h a i l

"I don't think the High Court is going to accept that. Even the Governor of the province stated that if Javed Iqbal does not appeal against that part, then the government will appeal on his behalf."

I thanked Mr. Minto and his wife and said goodbye. He asked me to call him if I needed any further assistance in my project.

On the way home, I was left with the distinct feeling that Mr. Minto was a very thoughtful but reserved man. Everything he said was stated with great precision. His thoughts, words and actions were very calculated and meaningful. I thought that if someone were filming his life, there would be no need for editing the results.

⌛ 7   A Visit to the Death Cell

After visiting the office of the Inspector General of Prisons I obtained my letter of permission to interview Javed Iqbal Mughal on April 7, 2000, in Kot Lakhpat Jail in the city of Lehore. When I mentioned that to Shoaib, he was quite willing to take a day off work and take me for the interview.

When we arrived at the Kot Lakhpat Jail, the gatekeeper stopped us, searched the car and asked dozens of unnecessary questions. Shoaib was irritated but I was amused. In those circumstances I always wonder why people working in institutions gradually lose their common sense. When I looked at the building, I saw high walls surrounded by electrified fencing, making it virtually impossible for prisoners to escape. Finally when the gatekeeper opened the door, he said, "You should hurry. Superintendent Sahib will be leaving in a few minutes."

"Stupid man!" Shoaib fumed. "If he was so worried, why was he wasting our time with all of his dumb questions?"

"He has to earn his living. Doing his duty, poor guy."

"But why at our expense?"

When we drove forward, we saw a white Mercedes and a few armed officers waiting for the Superintendent. Shoaib let me out and went to park the car. When I entered I saw the Superintendent coming out of his office and officers saluting him. I had no idea that a Superintendent of the prison was treated like an army general.

I rushed forward and presented the minister's letter. The Superintendent was very courteous. He took me back to his office and introduced me to his assistant.

"Shamsheer Khan! Dr. Sohail is here to interview Javed Iqbal. I am going to a meeting in Wapda House. Please take him to the death cell. He will be the visitor of the week."

"Yes, Sir!" Shamsheer Khan rose to his full height in respect.

The minister's letter had become the key that was opening many locked doors. I remembered telling Anne that the right contacts can make impossible things possible in Pakistan.

In the meantime Shoaib joined me. Shamsheer Khan asked him to remain in the waiting room and guided me towards the interior of the jail. First we passed through a large wooden door with old-fashioned metal locks. It seemed as though they had been made in the nineteenth century.

"How many prisoners do you have these days?"

"Nearly 2500, 2485 to be exact. The number changes every week."

"It is a big jail, bigger than some villages in Canada."

"It is a different world, a world of criminals." I agreed silently.

As we walked I looked around at a group of prisoners doing different tasks. Some were digging while others performed exercises. I was surprised to see Quranic verses all over the walls.

"When did these verses appear?" I asked Shamsheer Khan.

"During Zia-ul-Haq's regime. Everything became religious."

"Did it improve anything?"

"Yes, hypocrisy!" he said, catching the sarcasm of my question and we both laughed. That moment connected us at some deeper level and I felt more comfortable in that extremely uncomfortable environment.

"Shamsheer Sahib, what is your opinion about Javed Iqbal?"

"He is not an ordinary prisoner, Sir. He is very deep."

As we walked further I saw the sign of the Phansi Ghaat [the Death Cell].

"Do you use the electric chair?" I was curious.

"It is not Europe or America, Doctor. We tie a knot around the neck and pull the wooden board from under the feet."

"Are you in favor of capital punishment, Shamsheer Khan?"

"Doctor! You sound like a philosopher. For us it is a job. We work here to put bread and butter on the table for our children. We are poor people and we suffer day and night. We don't have time for idle discussions about human rights." Shamsheer Khan's voice had taken on a harder edge.

"I'm sorry I asked."

I had recently viewed the movie, *The Green Mile,* based on Stephen King's book, before leaving Toronto. Tom Hanks was in the lead role. Scenes of people burning in the electric chair were most disturbing and I hurriedly shut out the memory.

"You have one hour to interview Javed Iqbal," Shamsheer Khan said in a stern voice.

"That would not be enough to hear his life story."

"Such are the rules, Sir. Every prisoner gets one hour a day to walk and an hour a week for a visitor. You are the visitor of the week."

"Can I come back?"

"You can — if he is still alive."

As we moved forward, I saw the Phansi Ghaat on the left side and the three cells for the condemned on the right. Javed Iqbal was apparently in one of them, as an armed guard stood menacingly on each side of the entrance.

When I neared the death cell, I saw two chairs and a table set up on the verandah, obviously arranged for Javed Iqbal and me. While the officer was unlocking the cell, I saw through the bars a short, frail, bespectacled man reading a newspaper as he sat on his mattress on the floor. He looked calm and peaceful. Green *tasbeeh* [prayer beads] lay next to him.

"What is happening?" he asked the officer.

"A doctor is here to interview you."

"Which doctor? I am not expecting anyone." He did not look pleased.

What if he refuses to talk to me? I moved aside to give the officer time to open the cell door.

"You can sit outside," the officer said to me, "but it is hot in the sun. I can put your table and chair in his room. It is cool inside."

"Thank you," I answered. There was enough room in his cell for my chair and a small table. Javed Iqbal remained perplexed, not knowing what was being arranged. When I entered his cell, I saw a small room with paint peeling off the walls adding to its surrealistic appearance. In the front part of the room was a mattress on which Javed Iqbal lay. A wall separated us from the washroom facilities on the other side. After I sat on a chair in front of him I said, "My name is Dr. Khalid Sohail. I'm a psychiatrist from Canada and I have come all the way to meet with you. I have read the newspaper articles published about your case and also seen the court verdict. I feel as though the real story has not been told. I want to hear your story, which I think will be the real story. I want to know about your family of origin, your child-hood, your youth and everything important that took place before the present episode. I want to know the story behind the story."

As I was talking I could see him nodding his head. A connection was made. "I am glad you came to see me. I would like my story to be shared with the rest of the world. Maybe you will be able to do that. Maybe God sent you here with a definite purpose. You know God works in mysterious ways. I will share with you everything I know. I will not send you back disappointed." He took out a newspaper from under his pillow and asked me to read an article that stated that an organization in England was encouraging his lawyer to take his case to an interna-tional tribunal. They were willing to pay the lawyer's fee. Javed Iqbal told me that if that happened, it would be the first such case in the his-tory of Pakistan. It was obvious that my being from Canada was important to him. If I had come from a small village in Pakistan, I might not have received the same warm reception.

I set my papers and pen on the table and also removed my wrist-watch so that I could keep track of the short amount of time we had been allotted. Javed Iqbal watched me doing all that and settled in for a lengthy interview.

"Please start from the very beginning. Where were you born and what kind of family did you grow up in?"

"I was born in House No. 3, Ram Street No. 3, Nishtar Road,

which was also called Brandrath Road, Lahore in 1961. My father, Mian Mohammad Ali, was a businessman and a poet. He used to write *ghazals* [poems]. He liked visiting holy shrines. My maternal grandfather was also a well-respected holy man in his community. My mother, Zohra Perveen, was a housewife. Both of my parents were quite conservative and religious. My parents could not have any children in the early part of their marriage, so they adopted a son named Aijaz-ul-Haq. After the adoption, they had eight children of their own, four sons and four daughters. My brothers are Zia-ul-Haq, Pervaiz Iqbal and Saeed Mughal and my sisters are Shamshad Akhtar, Mumtaz Akhtar, Robina and Yasmeen. Yasmeen is also a poet like her father. All my brothers and sisters are married. I am the middle child."

"Tell me about your school days."

"I started in Mrs. Rasheeda Beg Primary School, which was very close to my house. I used to enjoy school but then ..."

At that moment Javed Iqbal became quiet. It seemed like a pregnant pause. I waited for him to talk again. "Dr. Sohail, now that you have come all the way from Canada, I want to share those parts of my life with you that I have not shared with others. I want you to really understand me and get to the root of the problem, get to the bottom of the story. People do not know the real story yet."

I was all ears. He took a deep breath and started again. "When I was about nine years old, something very special happened. I was in grade four at that time.

"I will never forget that afternoon. I had seen my father getting ready to go out, and I asked him, 'Where are you going, Dad?'

"'My son,' he said affectionately, 'a saint is visiting from Karachi and I am going to see him.'

"Can I come?" I begged him.

"Ask your mom. It is pretty hot out."

"When I asked Mom, she happened to be in a good mood. 'You can go if you wish,' she said. 'And ask Babaji to pray for you. He is a great saint. He can perform miracles.' She got me dressed and asked me to wear a cap to protect my head from the sun.

"So I went with my dad to the Holy Shrine where Babaji was going to address his disciples. The place was packed. I climbed over peoples' shoulders as they sat waiting, to get to the front row. I wanted to have a close look at the saint who performed miracles.

"Babaji came and sat in the seat of honour that was waiting for him. His clothes were as white as his long beard. There was a special glow in his eyes. He had a green tasbeeh in his right hand that I liked. I stared at the tasbeeh. I liked it so much that I wanted to have it and wear it around my neck."

Then Javed Iqbal picked up the tasbeeh that was lying next to his pillow, draped it around his neck and started talking again. "Babaji saw me staring at the rosary and smiled. His smile was as charming as his rosary.

"Babaji addressed his disciples for a long time or so it felt to me, as I did not understand most of what he said. Suddenly at one point he stopped talking, looked at me affectionately, smiled and asked his audience, 'Who is this child?'

'Javed Iqbal' someone replied.

'Who is his father?'

'Mian Mohammad Ali,' another answered.

'Call him.'

"And my father, climbing over peoples' shoulders, came forward and raised me off the mat and held me up to the mystic. Babaji said, 'I want to give you good news. Your son does not belong to this world. Look at his face, his eyes, his eyebrows. See the configuration of hair in the middle of his eyebrows. You will see a star. It is a sign, a sign of the heavenly world.'"

At that moment Javed Iqbal, (obviously in pain,) moved forward awkwardly, took off his glasses, and said, "Look here, in between my eyebrows you will see a sign. Most people either have a blank space or hair joining the eyebrows but I have three prongs. It is a star, a special sign from God."

It was as he said. His eyes were close to mine, seeking my approval. Javed Iqbal started talking again. "Then Babaji held my head in his two hands, closed his eyes and prayed. Suddenly I went into a trance and fell to the ground. When I got up, I was reciting verses from the Holy Quran.

"People in the audience were astonished to see the miracle. Babaji told my dad, 'Look after him. He will make the sick healthy. He has healing powers. He is special to God. He is "The Chosen One."

"After that encounter the saint started packing his belongings, getting ready to return to Karachi.

"But you have come to stay and preach sermons for two weeks," his disciples reminded him.

"I don't need to stay here now. Javed Iqbal will look after you people'. After that, the saint left and I remained in that altered state of consciousness for many months. During that time I went in and out of trances and talked in tongues and offered prophecies. People brought their sick children and I prayed for them and they got better. People started coming from far off places to get my blessings. I was as perplexed as others about all these miraculous happenings. Our whole family life got so disrupted that one day my mother asked my father, 'Why don't you take Javed Iqbal to Karachi to see Babaji and ask him to pray so that he does not enter these trances any more?' So Dad took me to Karachi.

"When Babaji saw us he said, 'I know why you are here. Please stay at the shrine for two days and then come to see me after Friday prayers.' So we stayed there with other disciples. I enjoyed living there, listening to *qawwalis* [musical get-togethers]. I would have loved to live there forever. It was so peaceful. When Dad took me back to Babaji after Friday prayers, he said, 'Mohammad Ali! I am asking one last time. Please leave your son here. I told you before, he does not belong to this world. He is "The Chosen One." God has blessed you with nine children, you can donate one back to him."

"My father had tears in his eyes. He said, 'Babaji! He is only nine. His mother loves him dearly. She will never forgive me if I leave him behind..'

"Then take him.' Babaji sounded angry with my father. 'But always remember one thing. He is not an ordinary boy. Don't force him to get married and lead a traditional life. And also make sure people do not hurt his feelings. If someone ever breaks his heart, there will be a big disaster. A curse will descend on the whole family and community, a curse similar to the communities of Noah and Lot. Beware of that day.'

"Dad brought me back home. I never had those trances again. I went back to school but I had special powers. I never forgot I was 'The Chosen One'.

"In school I excelled in everything I did.

"When I wanted to make speeches, I received prizes.

"When I wanted to sing, I was an excellent singer.

"When I wanted to paint, I felt as if I was in a trance and made beautiful oil paintings.

"When I wanted to do *qirat* [recitation of Quran], everybody admired my recitation.

"I was very successful as a student. But my heart was in writing. I wanted to be a journalist, that was my passion. I wanted to reform society, change it, transform it and I thought journalism was the best way to do it. My articles were published in the newspaper 'Waqt' [Time] even when I was in grade 7. I have kept a record of all those articles. If you ever meet my writer sister Yasmeen Yaas, she can show them to you. She lives on 144 Sher Shah Road, Shad Bagh Lahore. She also has all my oil paintings."

"Did any of your teachers mistreat or abuse you?"

"Yes, there was one. His name was Master Riaz. He was fat and ugly and cruel. He was also the teacher of my older brother Aijaz-ul-Haq and did not like him either. He seemed revengeful and always tormented me. Nobody liked him. We went to his house for special tutoring to be in his good books but even that did not work. Finally it got so bad that one day when he was teaching us, one of my friends, Bholla, threw kerosene on the door and put a match to it. We all ran and saved our lives. Master Riaz was really angry. He blamed me for the whole incident. He thought I had set Bholla up but that was not true. I was upset as I was wrongfully accused. That made me angry and bitter. Finally when I appeared in the exam, my marks were in the 90s in all the subjects except two subjects that were taught by Master Riaz. I had not appeared in those two papers as a protest. The authorities got concerned and investigated the case. I was given a special certificate exempting me from those two papers and Master Riaz lost his job because of his abusive behaviour. Since then I have known that anyone who wanted to hurt me got destroyed.

"In high school, I also had other interests. I used to collect old coins and stamps. I was also very fond of pen-friendships. I was an unusual child. I never played in the street with other kids. I never played cricket or football. I never watched TV. I was very solitary, a loner. I enjoyed my own company. I was more connected with people in far off places than my own neighbours. I used to write letters to my penfriends all over the world. I even had planned to bring out a magazine with the help of my friend Zahid in Saudi Arabia. It was called "Javed International". I had invited all my penfriends to put their names and addresses in it so that we could make an international network of friends. I had a desire to know people from all over the world. It gave me a lot of satisfaction.

"After graduating from Muslim High School I went to Islamia College, Railway Road. Those were the days I got interested in world religions. I registered in an institution in Faisalabad and studied the Old and New Testament and other Holy Scriptures. I appeared in their exam and received three certificates."

"How did your formal studies end?"

"I was in college that time, it was the late 70s and I got involved in a protest against Zulfiqar Ali Bhutto. There was a confrontation with the police and I got so badly injured that I had to be admitted to the hospital. It took me a long time to recover and I could not continue my college studies. I left college and got involved in business."

Suddenly an officer appeared with bread and food in a bucket and offered Javed Iqbal his meal.

"Would you like to eat with me?" he asked.

"No thanks, I would like to finish the interview."

"Can you leave my food in the next cell with Sajid. I will eat later." [Sajid was the teenager who was also going to be hanged as he was convicted of killing 98 children with Javed Iqbal.] After dismissing the officer, he looked at me, waiting for the next question.

"What about your marriages?"

"I got married twice because of the pressures of my family. They did not last. They failed badly. The saint had told my father not to put pressure on me to get married but he did not listen. That is why there was a big disaster. I have not seen my wives or children for years. I have one child from each wife."

Suddenly Javed Iqbal became quiet. Then he said, "I am in pain. Terrible pain. I was beaten up so badly three years ago that I was in hospital, unconscious for twenty-two days. They had killed me. But I survived. It is a miracle that I survived. But I am a dead man. I can hardly walk. They give me half an hour twice a day for my walk and I cannot walk without support. My backbone is broken. I do not have crutches. So I ask Sajid to give me help. I put my hand on his shoulders and walk." Then he looked at me intently and said, "Give me your hand."

It was quite unexpected for me. I was facing a man who had been convicted of killing a hundred children. I knew two security officers were outside the death cell but I could not see them.

"Should I give him my hand or not?" I asked myself. If I give him my hand, I will take a big risk. But if I do not, I will betray his trust. I suddenly had a flashback from the movie *Silence of the Lambs* in which Anthony Hopkins plays a serial killer and kills the man who shakes hands with him in his cell. I felt a cold shiver run down my spine.

"Would he hurt me?" I asked myself again.

My heart whispered he would not. In some strange way I trusted this serial killer.

So I extended my arm. He held my hand and with my index finger touched his forehead, cheekbone and jaw. I could feel the dents, the fractures. He was, without doubt, a broken man. Before letting my hand go, he lingered for a few seconds. His touch was not aggressive, was not sexual, it was sensual. At that moment I wondered whether he was homosexual or just deprived of human touch.

"They killed me," he said. "But I am still alive. They cannot kill me. Human beings can control everything in life except two things; birth and death. They are in God's Hands."

"They have given me only an hour to interview you. I am already overtime."

"Just relax, Doctor. Do not worry. I have told them, 'Do not mess around with me.' I am full of fractures in the skull, in my jaw and in my backbone. I can hit my head against the brick wall a few times and I will die and the prison people will be in a big mess. So relax and ask questions."

Suddenly Javed Iqbal was transformed in front of my eyes. The man who, in his gentleness, was posing as a saint and a mystic and a reformer had anger and disgust in his eyes. His dark side was coming out.

"Tell me a little bit about your employment."

"I ran a factory for eight years. I used to sell metal pipes. Pathans used to come to buy them and make pistols. I also brought out a magazine focusing on anti-corruption activities. People used to come and tell me stories especially about their children who ran away from home. I was always very critical of the police."

"Did you ever have unusual experiences? Did you ever see or hear extraordinary things?" The psychiatrist in me did not want to miss an opportunity for a clinical question.

"Yes, once someone did Black Magic. I woke up in the middle of the night quite disturbed. When I looked outside I could see every vein of every leaf of the tree. Then I saw smoke coming out. That magic stayed for quite a while and I saw smoke coming out for a few days. I think my mother-in-law did that. My in-laws never liked me."

As I looked outside the cell I saw an officer. He had come to tell me that I had to leave. I asked Javed Iqbal if I could come back. He said, "You are more than welcome anytime. And if you want to see my paintings and articles please go to 144 Shadbagh and you will find more things. Thank you for coming all the way from Canada to listen to my story."

When Shoaib and I were leaving, I thanked Shamsheer Khan and asked him, "Can you give me my letter back?"

"Which letter?" He looked perplexed.

"The minister's letter that I brought for the Superintendent."

"That letter will be saved in our files."

"I need a copy of that letter."

"For what?" He still looked lost.

"For my own file."

"But I cannot make a copy for you."

"Why not?"

"We do not have a photocopying machine." We both fell quiet for a while. I was used to having a phone, fax and e-mail facilities at my fingertips in my clinic in Canada. I could have never imagined that a jail with 2500 prisoners in a country of over 100 million people would not have a photocopier.

"Doctor Sahib! I can do one thing."

"What is that?"

"I can send our officer Alaf Khan with you to town and he can get a photocopy made of your letter."

"That is a good idea. Thanks."

Shoaib asked Alaf Khan to come with us. As we were driving, I said to Shoaib, "I am sorry I kept you waiting for so long."

"Don't worry, I was quite amused."

"Amused with what?"

"I watched prisoners meeting their relatives. It seemed as if the prisoners were inside and the relatives outside the cage. They could see and talk but could not touch each other." Then he looked at Alaf Khan and asked, "May I ask you a question?"

"Go ahead."

"Why was it that some visitors were asked to leave after half an hour while others could stay longer?"

Alaf Khan laughed and said, "Do you want to know the truth?"

"Of course."

"Those visitors who give the officers a hundred-rupee gift can stay longer." I chuckled to myself hearing a bribe being called a gift.

8 The Magic of the Black Box and Pakistani Politics

It was good to be out in the busy streets, away from the oppressive atmosphere of the prison. Shoaib and I were hungry, so our search for a likely spot to have lunch ended in a place that served kebabs. We settled down at a table in the shade with cold drinks and Shoaib's newspaper. The headlines stated that the court had handed down two life sentences to former Prime Minister of Pakistan, Nawaz Sharif. I was quite surprised.

"That would ruin his political career," I commented.

"Oh, yes. Do you know what happened?"

"No—I follow the news as best I can, but you would know the real story."

"It is not easy to summarize in a few sentences. There was a major conflict between the army and the government. To have or not have war with India was the underlying issue. So when Pervez Musharaf, the army Chief of Staff, went to Sri Lanka for a visit, Nawaz Sharif fired him in his absence. When Pervez Musharaf returned to Pakistan and his plane was about to land at Karachi airport, the control tower refused to let them land. Along with Pervez Musharaf, there were also nearly 300 civilian passengers on that plane. Luckily, he had his cell phone with him, and he was able to talk to his generals and find out what was happening. He ordered them to take over the airport and the country and arrest Nawaz Sharif. Then once Pervez Musharaf was in power, he had Nawaz Sharif charged with attempting to kill 300 innocent citizens."

"But how did they prove it?"

"With the help of the magical Black Box!"

"They are amazing, aren't they. Like peoples' unconscious, they are full of secrets. What did the Black Box reveal?"

"The pilot told the control tower that he had only seven minutes worth of fuel left, but the control tower said that the Prime Minister had ordered them not to let the plane land anyway."

"Hard to believe somebody could do a thing like that!"

The kebabs, salad and naans arrived, and we tucked into them with good appetite.

"People in the West were baffled when people in Pakistan celebrated the changeover. They still cannot believe a nation would prefer an army dictator to a democratically elected Prime Minister. Why do you think people are so happy about a military dictatorship?"

"It is because people believe Pervez Musharaf is not a dictator and Nawaz Sharif was not a democratic person. They were worried that Nawaz Sharif was walking in the footsteps of the Taliban of Afghanistan. They perceived him as a corrupt leader. They feel that Pervez Musharaf is an honest and liberal person. Actually, they were expecting that Nawaz Sharif would be hanged like Zulfiqar Ali Bhutto, when Zia-ul-

Haq took over. What a strange coincidence that Zulfiqar Ali Bhutto had also been incarcerated in Kot Lakpath jail before he was hanged.

"I have talked to a lot of people who would like to see Benazir Bhutto back."

"That's true. They think she is liberal and socialist minded."

"Do you remember when her father Zulfiqar Ali Bhutto took over the government?"

"No, I was too small then."

"He was the one who started the Islamization process of Pakistan. He misled people with his slogans: 'Islam is our religion, Socialism is our economy, Democracy is our politics.' Gradually Socialism and Democracy went into the background and Islam came to the forefront. The left wing liberal intellectuals and politicians were disappointed when Bhutto was intimidated by the right wing *mullahs* [priests]. To please them he banned alcohol, made Friday the weekly holiday and finally declared Ahmedis as non-Muslims."

"But Pervez Musharaf is not like that. He is quite secular minded."

"But he will not succeed. The hold of religious groups is gradually increasing throughout the country. Last week when a minister said that he wanted to see Pakistan a secular state, he had to retract his statement the next day."

"I feel Pervez Musharaf wants to pave the way for genuine democracy in Pakistan." Shoaib was clinging to his hopes.

"It will never happen. Democracy does not prosper in a religious environment. It needs a secular atmosphere. As long as Pakistan is the Islamic Republic of Pakistan, we can forget about democracy, socialism and secularism. For democracy you need dialogues, but in a religious state we hear only monologues."

We finished our lunch in silence. I could fly back to Canada, but Shoaib had to remain, living under the latest set of masters in an increasingly religious environment.

The next morning Shoaib arrived early to have breakfast. He called his friend Abid to get directions to Javed Iqbal's family's house, as he was not familiar with the area. While driving to Shadbagh we passed through the chamra mandi, a market where we saw thousands of shops in which men were cleaning, drying and tanning cow hides. Shoaib told me that those skins were exported to the four corners of the world to make leather goods.

"But where do they get all those skins?" I asked him.

"Muslims love meat," he said. "Especially during celebrations. On Eid thousands of cows and sheep are sacrificed and their skins donated to mosques to help the poor. All those skins land up in this market."

"I am glad Hindus don't live here, otherwise there would have been World War III every day in this market."

We passed through the old part of Lahore where the streets were dusty and crowded. Nobody followed the traffic laws. I was amazed how within a few days I was getting used to unclean air and water and food as if I had never left Pakistan. Maybe it was because I had never lived in a smoke free environment even in Canada. I always believed that a few impurities in life were natural and healthy. Those Pakistanis who lived like other Canadians and were obsessed with cleanliness usually got sick when they visited Pakistan. I thought if the whole world is becoming a global village, the villagers need to develop global personalities, personalities that are comfortable in different environments and cultures. While I was lost in the labyrinth of my thoughts, Shoaib asked, "What was the street address Javed Iqbal gave you?'

"144 Shadbagh."

Finally Shoaib found the street and parked the car. I was amazed that anybody could park the car anywhere without worrying about getting a ticket or the car being towed away.

As we walked in the street, we were surprised to see the numbers on the houses 144A, 144B, and 144C. I rang the bell of 144B and a teenager cautiously opened the door.

"I am Dr. Sohail," I said, "I am a writer and I would like to talk to the poetess Miss Yasmeen Yaas."

"There is no Yasmeen Yaas in this house!" He closed the door before I could ask him any more questions. Shoaib knocked on the other two doors with similar results.

"Does she not live there or do they do not want us to talk to her?" I wondered.

While we were standing on the corner wondering what to do next, a middle-aged woman, wearing a traditional *burqa* [veil], came out of house number 144A and approached me.

"Which Yasmeen Yaas are you looking for?"

"She is a poetess and sister of Javed Iqbal who was accused of murdering 100 children." I was open and honest.

"Oh," she said. "You are looking for Javed Iqbal's family. You are in the wrong Shadbagh. This is the old one. If you go straight and turn left you will find yourself in the New Shadbagh. They live there."

We thanked the lady and went to the place she suggested and found a market. When we went inside, I approached a young bearded man and asked him about Javed Iqbal's family.

"Who are you?" he asked.

"I am Dr. Sohail, a psychiatrist from Canada. Javed Iqbal suggested I contact you people."

'I am Saeed, Javed Iqbal's younger brother. But where did you meet Javed Iqbal?" He looked puzzled.

"In the prison. I met with him and interviewed him about his situation, and he suggested I meet with you."

"Okay, I will inform my family."

Then Saeed took us a to room off the shop and asked us to wait while he consulted the family. Time passed and nobody came. I could imagine them wondering who I was and what my motives were. No doubt they had been in the glare of public scrutiny since the trial and would be wary of strangers coming to discuss the whole thing again. I had almost given up on them, when Saeed reappeared with some of his family in tow. He introduced them as his older brother, sister and nephews. They offered us drinks and gracefully agreed to be interviewed. The room was partially open to the street and there was a slight breeze.

When everybody had been seated, I turned to Pervez Iqbal, a tall slim man with a short moustache, who had been introduced as Javed Iqbal's elder brother.

"I have made this journey to try to understand how your brother came to be who he is ... to find out the background to the present situation. I truly appreciate you and your family agreeing to talk to me. To start with, can you tell me about your ancestors and the family background you grew up in?"

"We belong to a religious family," he said, "The family is not narrow-minded or prejudiced, it is rather spiritual. Our father was a very hard-working man. He always tried to earn an honest living. He worked hard and God rewarded him. There were times he worked 24 hours straight only taking two to three hours break to have some sleep. My grandfather and great-grandfather were from Jalandhar. They were rich but then they lost their wealth. We are from a Mughal family. The crisis with Mughals was that at first they were suppressed by the British and later resented by the Hindus because they were Muslims. Because of those circumstances many Mughals were deprived of education. We were lucky to have some education and acquired some social status. Our family was involved in the steel industry and that is how they earned their living.

"Spiritually speaking, we belong to the Chishti Sabri tradition. Our maternal grandfather had a holy shrine. Before the tragedy, Javed Iqbal used to go there to meditate. My mother belonged to that simple saintly family. They were all nice, gentle people. There was never any vulgarity in the family.

"Tell me about your father and his marriages."

"When my dad got married the first time, he did not have any children. Then he married our mother and he still did not have any children. On some older person's suggestion, he adopted a son. Then, like a miracle, he had his own children. Most people would not believe the story of how that came to be. What happened was that a saint, Sain Ruknuddin, who had a shrine in Jaranwala, came to visit my parents. My father brought out a basket of fruit and the saint handed my mother an orange. He told her to peel it and count the segments. There were nine. The saint said that she would have nine children. Later on the prophecy of that saint came true. We never met that saint but we heard this story from our mother.

"Javed Iqbal also experienced a miracle when he was scarcely ten. He was in school at that time. He was known as an intelligent child. When the saint came from Karachi and met Javed Iqbal, he put his hand on Javed's head and Javed went into a trance. The saint covered him with a green cloth. After that Javed started making prophecies which came true. We witnessed those things with our own eyes but we were children then. We thought he was staging a drama and making excuses not to go to school. We did not know the truth. The saint went back to Karachi but Javed kept on going into trances. Gradually Dad realized it was becoming a problem. This went on for a few months. Whenever he made prophecies, they came true. Only God knows the real truth — for us it was a big game. Finally Dad took Javed Iqbal to Karachi to meet with the same saint.

"Dad said, 'Because of Javed Iqbal, our family is facing a lot of problems. You have opened a Pandora's box....'

"The saint said, 'God has given you so many children, you should donate one to God. He will serve humanity. Leave him with us.' Dad responded, 'I cannot afford to donate a son to God and the holy shrine. I feel responsible for his future. I am just an ordinary man. Please let him lead an ordinary life.'

"The saint said, 'If we can't have him you won't be able to have him either.' He said those profound words.

"When Javed came back from Karachi he started behaving normally and resumed his schooling. He was quite bright and creative. He was involved in many extra-curricular activities. He used to write columns in the newspapers and take part in debates. He was very successful in those activities. Those days we used on live on Ram Gali No 3 on Brandrath Road and Javed Iqbal used to go to Muslim High School No. 1.

"Our father had a philosophy that when children reach adulthood, they should be married off so that they do not get into trouble. So my two brothers and one sister got married at the same time. They were provided a separate place to live and separate businesses so that they could start their independent lives. At that time my brothers were seventeen and eighteen. Javed was nearly thirteen at that time. When older brothers got married and left home, Javed was left without supervision. After a year and a half, I got married and left the family home. I moved to Shadbagh and opened a workshop. We used to fix pipes. Dad asked me to train Javed. He worked with me for a while but then we had a conflict. When I shared the problem with Dad he suggested that I hand over the workshop to Javed and take over his business on Brandrath Road.

"After I moved to Brandrath Road and got busy with my own business and family, I lost touch with Javed and then he got into trouble. Everybody is aware of the social problems we have in our community. We all know how children are abused in the mosques and other places and how people get involved in crime. Javed got involved in bad company too. One important factor in his life was his failed marriage."

"Tell me about his marriage. How old was he when he got married for the first time?"

"When Javed Iqbal got married he was nearly seventeen years old. He was young. He was beautiful. He was running a business and he was from a well-respected family. He was also a volunteer worker in the community. He always tried to help people. He was also involved in the Business Association. When a certain family liked him, they talked to him about their daughter and he agreed. So it was going to be neither an arranged nor a love marriage. But our family disagreed with the arrangement, as we had a tradition of encouraging our children to marry within the family. We are from a Mughal family and he wanted to marry a girl from Qureshi family. Our family asked Javed Iqbal not to marry outside the family, but he insisted. At one point he threatened that if the family would not agree then he would commit suicide. One of our uncles talked to the elders and suggested that for his happiness we should agree with his proposal. So the family finally gave in and the wedding was planned. The ceremony was a memorable one. A lot of dignitaries from the community were invited for the wedding and all the neighbors were welcomed — nobody needed a formal invitation. We hoped they would be happy together.

"But then something went wrong. Maybe someone did voodoo or black magic, God knows what, but they had problems in the marriage.

In the beginning we did not realize the source of the conflict. Later on we found out that Javed's in-laws lived in Saudi Arabia and since Javed Iqbal's wife was the eldest, she was asked to look after the younger children. She asked Javed Iqbal to become *ghar jawi* [live in his in-laws' house] which he found humiliating. When he did not agree to her proposal, she went back to her family and a gap appeared between spouses. So a newly married man became single all over again.

"Being a newly-married man he must have had some physical needs and when they were not met in the marriage, maybe he went astray. In his workshop he had some young boys who were his employees. Maybe after the marital crisis his criminal tendencies came to the surface and finally led to the present disaster. As far as our family is concerned we do not have a history of criminality. There is nothing genetic. All the crimes he committed were the result of being brought up in this environment. He returned to his society what he got from them."

"When did you find out that he was sexually abusing children?"

"In 1990 he was charged with sodomy. It was hell for the whole family. We faced the same tragedy as we are facing now. I used to work on Brandrath road those days. One morning when my dad and I were working in our shop some people attacked our home. At that time only the women of our family were there. Those people who came and attacked were Pathans and they were armed. When they found out that we men were at work they came to our shop on Brandrath Road. Those days all the brothers used to meet at Dad's shop first and then go to our shops. Those people came and attacked us. Then they forced us to go with them in a rickshaw. We had no idea where were they taking us. When we saw the Police Station of Shadbagh we felt relieved. We were afraid they were going to kidnap us and torture us.

"There, the police told us about the incident of Javed Iqbal sodomizing a boy. Those people were shouting and screaming and cursing and swearing. Our dad was a gentle soul. He had never been inside a police station in his whole life. When he heard the story of his son, he lowered his head with shame and embarrassment. After that incident, for the rest of his life he could not raise his head with pride.

Dr. K. Sohail

"We were kept in police custody for a week. Those people used to come and swear at us. They asked us where Javed Iqbal was, as he had run away in the meanwhile."

"Did the case involve another adult or a child?"

"He was involved with a child. We used to warn him to stay away from the children. We did not want him to get into trouble again. We used to ask parents not to let their boys hang around with him. We told them his character was not good. After the incident we used to keep our boys away from him. After a week of being in police custody, the women of our family met with the women of their family and told them that if there was a crime it was committed by Javed Iqbal and not by us. We were innocent. They should let us free so that we could help them find Javed Iqbal. Finally they saw our point and asked the police to release us. After being released from police custody we tried to find him.

"Finally we found that thirteen-year-old boy who was living with him at that time. When we got that boy into custody, then we knew we would be able to catch Javed Iqbal. You have to understand that Javed Iqbal is a strange creature and he has strange relationships with those boys. If someone killed his family, he would not be upset but if someone cursed one of his boys he would go crazy with anger and fight on their behalf. In this present case, police tried their best but his boys took his side. They might be hanged in the process but they are still faithful to him. They are so faithful that the whole world is astonished.

"Anyway, when we got that boy arrested, then sure enough, Javed appeared on the scene. We found out that he had gone to see Gul Asghar, Superintendent of Police of Qilla Gujar Singh, so we went there looking for him. When he saw us, he took us into the Superintendent's office and told us all that he was the victim of false accusations. The Superintendent told him that he should hand himself over to the police and if the accusations were false then we could help him clear himself. We brought him home and talked to him, but he was unwilling to turn himself in. Finally we locked him up in one room and called the police. At that time Malik Shahab-ud-din Aawaan was Sergeant. He came to Brandrath Road with his officers and arrested Javed.

"Because of that crisis, because we had all been in jail, Dad's business was closed for a week and when people asked him where he had disappeared, he felt ashamed and embarrassed. He was so upset that he suffered a heart attack. He did not die with that attack, and he gradually recovered. Javed Iqbal was sentenced to six months in jail. My dad spent a lot of money to fight the case in court and get him out of jail. While Javed Iqbal was in jail he wrote him letters. My father was such a gentleman he even addressed his sons with respect. He never became bitter.

"Javed Iqbal insisted that he had been charged on political grounds. He said because he was involved in local politics and the affairs of the Business Association, he was targeted unjustly. He said his in-laws had framed him because they did not like him anymore. My parents who were soft hearted, believed him. My dad spent thousands of rupees to get him legal help. Finally, based on some technicalities in court he was set free.

"When Javed Iqbal came out of jail, my dad was worried that he might get involved in homosexual encounters again, so we tried to mend his marriage. The whole family put their heads together. We approached his wife many times but she refused to go back to him. She said she hated him. She even had a daughter from that marriage. We even approached Doctor Bangash who was MP [Member of Parliament] at that time to help us. He met with both families many times but the wife did not agree. She said she would give him permission to have a second marriage. Her father in the presence of the MP gave his word that they would have no objection if Javed Iqbal had a second wife.

"The boys who worked with Javed Iqbal introduced him to another woman who found a wife for him. Later on we found out that his new father-in-law was involved in illegal drug business. He used to come to harass Javed to get money. That created tension in the family and it wasn't long until divorce was being discussed. Within six months the second marriage also failed. This happened in 1992. Because of all that, Dad was so upset that he had another heart attack and finally died on July 17th, 1992.

"After Dad's death, the family got into real difficulties over the inheritance. The hostilities started even during his funeral ceremony. How to divide property was the main disputed question. Dad used to handle all the business and legal matters himself. Our brothers-in-law became suspicious of what he had arranged, so they challenged the will. In that process when we found out that our sisters had to appear in court, of course we didn't want that, so we urged the judge to finalize the case as quickly as possible. Finally our mother was consulted and the case was closed. We wanted to give Javed Iqbal all that he deserved and then keep a distance from him. We wanted him to handle his own affairs and face the consequences of his actions. We did not want to be embarrassed and humiliated because of his lifestyle. We had seen what had happened to our dad and we did not want to repeat the same mistake again.

"When Javed Iqbal got his share of the inheritance he bought real estate in Rana Town from Shaikh Nasir, the fellow he has mentioned in his diary. He used to be my classfellow and I was the one who introduced him to my younger brother. He was very affectionate with Javed Iqbal. Nasir wanted to make a deal with him, take the shop on Brandrath road and give him a Pejaro car and some property in Rana Town. So they made that deal but afterwards Javed realized that he had been tricked. That created bad feelings in their relationship. Javed felt he had really been taken for a ride. He used to express his bitterness about the deal.

"On his property in Rana Town he built a beautiful residence with a fancy swimming pool. It was in the wilderness and not very safe. Many people got attacked and mugged there. So he got scared and sold his property. Then he decided to start a new business and set up video centers in different places. He always had businesses that involved children and we never approved of that. We used to tell him that either he should live with his wife or when he came to visit us he should not bring boys with him. He used to say, 'These boys cook for me, look after me and help me in my videogame business.' I was dead set against his lifestyle so I never went to see any of his video centers. The only time I saw one of them was in his Fatehgarh residence on the occasion of a special religious ceremony he had organized in the memory of our father. Of course I went there to be part of that. This was in '97 or '98".

He paused after his long narration to take a drink of juice. The rest of the family sat watching us, and I could not read their faces. I noticed too that a number of the neighbors had quietly come in and were leaning against the wall and sitting on boxes listening to the story.

He continued, "When we arrived we were surprised to see a number of police cars and officers in uniform. We got nervous because we thought he had been involved in another crime. We stopped the car and were going to turn around and leave but he saw us and waved us to come in. We sent our son to find out what was happening. He told us that the police officers were all his friends. We went in by the back where he had the video centre, and stayed away from the police as much as we could. After a couple of hours those officers left. We had seen him socializing with them many times. The police were quite involved in his life because he also used to publish a magazine about them. We never approved of his involvement with them. Our Dad did not approve of it either. He used to say, 'Law abiding citizens need not socialize with the police.' But he was always close to them. He even used to get their help for others who were in legal trouble. After moving to Rana Town he had a good business and he established himself there."

"You had mentioned that the police were involved a second time. Can you share that with me?"

"That incident took place after he was charged again with sodomy. That happened in 1997. He thought that his friends Nasim Murshad and others that he has mentioned in his diaries would come to help him but they did not. Javed Iqbal said that the people who had him charged owed him money, and when he demanded his money back, they made false accusations and framed him in a sodomy charge. Since he had been charged before with the same offence, it was easy to make another case. He thought the way his dad had helped him in his 1990 case, the family would help him this time too, but we refused to help him. We wanted him to learn a lesson and change his lifestyle. Since we did not help him, he had to spend his own money to get out of trouble. Gradually the distance between him and the family increased."

At that point Pervez Iqbal had to go to attend to business but he gave me a pile of newspaper articles and police reports and as well, Javed Iqbal's diaries to read. He was quite willing for me to come back and talk to him again. I thanked him profusely and he left to go back to work. When I looked around I saw Javed Iqbal's sister standing there listening to our conversation with tears in her eyes. I had never seen such a quiet but profound expression of a sister's love.

"Javed Iqbal asked me to see his paintings and newspaper articles. Can you show them to me?" I asked her.

"I am sorry, I can't. The police confiscated them all."

I said my good-byes to the family and left, planning to spend an evening reading the intriguing material given to me by Javed Iqbal's brother.

Before settling down to read, I sent Anne an e-mail to update her on my progress and plans.

Dear Anne!

You would be pleased to know that not only was I able to interview Javed Iqbal in his death cell, I was also successful in talking to his family. Mr. Minto was a great help in getting me special permission to do the interview, while my cousin Shoaib was very helpful in taking me around the city. He knows a number of influential people in town, which makes my life easier. Since I am planning to go back to interview Javed Iqbal one more time, I would appreciate it if you would cancel my appointments for one more week. Now that I have started this project, I would like to get as much information as possible to solve this mystery. The story is far more convoluted and intriguing than I originally thought. I will send you the first drafts of my interviews and I look forward to your comments. E-mail has made life so much easier. Now we don't have to wait for weeks to get mail! You don't need to worry about me. I am safe and well looked after.

Sincerely,
Sohail

Sodomy and Pubic Humiliation:
   Interview with Ariff Butt (Neighbour)

While I was poring over the articles and diaries that night, Shoaib called me to ask me if I would like to interview Javed Iqbal's neighbours. They had known him all his life and would have valuable insights to offer.

This was a stroke of unbelievable good luck. "How did you make contact?" I asked him. "You don't know them."

"My friend Abid, who lives in that area knows them and I asked him to talk to them. He says they are willing to be interviewed."

I was keen to fill in more pieces of the puzzle. "Can you arrange it for tomorrow?" The ever-obliging Shoaib called his friend again and the arrangements were made.

The next day, Shoaib picked me up after he had finished work and took me back to Shadbagh. By this time Shoaib was quite familiar with the directions.

Unfortunately, familiarity definitely did breed contempt; this time we sped through the streets with a fine disregard for the rules of the road, whatever they may have been. People, horse-drawn carts and bicycles scattered to both sides, until finally we pulled up smartly in front of the Shadbagh Market. We looked for a certain video store and upon entering, met three gentlemen who were there waiting to see us.

INTERVIEW WITH ARIFF BUTT

The store was owned by Arif Butt, a pleasant young man. He bade us welcome and introduced us to a short man named Shahbaz and a tall heavy-set man with a long beard named Aslam Darvesh. I introduced myself and thanked them for coming.

After the formalities, I started my interview with Ariff Butt. "Can you tell me something about yourself and how you came to know Javed Iqbal?"

"Well, for the last twenty years I have been the General Secretary of the Shadbagh Market Association. I have known Javed Iqbal since

1985. We used to be neighbors at one time but I did not know him very well then. Then he came to this market and he started to sell video games. He used to be quite active socially. Once he arranged a flea market here and invited a Minister for the opening ceremony.

"I remember the time his case was presented before the council. I was the Secretary and Khawaja Mukhtar was the President. When we investigated, we found out that he had sexually abused a boy. We called the parties involved and we asked Javed Iqbal to apologize publicly. He went from one shop to another in the market to apologize for his actions and then we asked him to leave the area for six months. We even asked him to give us this undertaking in writing on a *Shtam* [legal paper]. That paper used to be kept with Khawaja Mukhtar who unfortunately is now deceased. After that incident we never saw Javed Iqbal for one year. At that time he was in his late teens. He was already married and was having marital problems."

"Tell me about his marriage."

"He lived close to the post office. He had a pipe factory there where his brothers have erected a plaza now. He belonged to a gentle and well respected family. Over there he got to know a woman who later on became his mother-in-law. There was some discussion of marriage and then it was all decided. We all attended his wedding, which was arranged with great pomp and show. After a while when they separated, we were curious about the reason for it. We thought he must have done something drastically wrong for her to leave him. It is such a delicate matter that one cannot ask questions openly. We all tried to help them reconcile. She went back to him once but then left him again.

"Afterwards when he was charged again with sexually abusing a boy, he left this area and we rarely saw him after that. We also found out that his brother-in-law told him that he was becoming a source of embarrassment for the family.

"After leaving this area he bought a big plot in Imamia Colony in Ferozpur and started living there. About two or three years ago, we found out that he was in hospital. His nephew Nadeem told me that he had hired someone from *Data Darbar* [Data Holy Shrine] to give him a massage and that boy had hit him over the head and run away with his money. I thought there must be more to the story.

"About three weeks later when I met Nadeem again, he told me that Javed Iqbal had regained consciousness and had returned home. During that time his father had passed away too.

"When we heard that he had written a letter to police confessing that he had killed one hundred children, we did not believe it. As long as we have known him he was always a coward. He was never brave. I knew that he liked horror movies. In those days horror movies were not very common but he was crazy about them. He liked action and violence in the movies. We never believed that he could kill one hundred children. It was true though, that he liked melodrama in his life. He liked guns as he worked with Pathans and supplied them with pipes for their pistols.

"When we heard that he had gone into hiding, we were sure that the police would never be able to catch him. One day, when he decided, he would surrender voluntarily. And that was what actually happened in the end. The police kept his brothers and nephews in custody while they were searching for him. His family asked us to help them but we were helpless. It wasn't some ordinary court case; it was about the murder of one hundred children. But we are sure he could never kill one hundred children. Maybe one or two but not a hundred.

"I remember once, that after sexually abusing a boy, he had left him in the park unconscious. The child's family found their son there. They took him to the hospital. When the child recovered he told them that a man took him to his house and then sexually abused him. After all, children are naive and innocent. They cannot express those experiences correctly. After that incident we stopped socializing with him because it was humiliating for us.

"Among all his brothers he had the most money. His father loved him a lot and gave him lots of money. He used to associate a lot with Pathans and we used to say, 'He likes Pathans and enjoys homosexual activities.'

"We thought that if he really killed one hundred children, how come there is no independent evidence? He must be really smart! Last night I met my friend Maqsood Heera who is a journalist with Jang newspaper. He asked me if I wanted to go and see Javed Iqbal. I told him, 'I don't even want to see his face. He is such a filthy man. I cannot imagine even looking at him.'

"It is also strange that on one hand he made confessions that he killed one hundred children and then when he went to court he denied them. He keeps on contradicting himself. Killing one hundred children is not some ordinary thing!"

INTERVIEW WITH SHAHBAZ (Colleague)

After hearing Arif Butt's account, I turned to Shahbaz and asked him, "What do you recall of Javed Iqbal?"

He replied, "I've been a businessman in this community for the last twenty-five years. These days I work in Meraj Deen Tailor's Shop. I met Javed Iqbal in 1985. Those days I used to be in charge of Tahir Shahbaz Library. He used to come to borrow books and magazines. He liked magazines with criminal stories and also mystery digests. From the very beginning I did not like him. Then he started up a videogame business. In those days I used to install and repair videogames.

One day when I was repairing one of those videogames for him, I witnessed an incident that I want to share with you. While some children were playing with videogames there in his shop, he threw a hundred rupee bill on the floor. One of the boys picked it up and put it in his pocket. Then Javed Iqbal asked the boys, "I have lost a hundred rupee bill. Has anybody picked it up?" All the boys denied it. Then he said, "I am going to search all of you. He knew which boy had picked it up, so he searched him last. I kept on working quietly and watching this game. Then he asked that boy to go next door to his house, which in those days was adjacent to his store. At that time I did not realize why he took the boy to his home. After a while I found out that he sexually abused those boys. Mr. Arif Butt just shared with you that once, after abusing a boy he had simply dumped him in the park. These incidents are part of the same chain. They reflect his personality and his mentality. He was a criminal from the very beginning." He shook his head in disgust.

INTERVIEW WITH ASLAM DARVESH
(President of Business Association)

I turned to the older gentleman, Mohammad Aslam Darvesh, and asked him, "Would you tell me something about yourself and your impressions of Javed Iqbal."

He responded, "I have been the President of the Shadbagh Market Association for the last thirty years. I was also the Secretary before I became the President. Javed Iqbal grew up in this area. He is more of a narcissistic person than a criminal. He tries to promote himself by exaggerating things. In the beginning we were not aware of this side of his personality. He used to come to us with the idea of having a flea market and once he actually arranged one, and invited the Minister of Food for the opening ceremony. But we knew he was a corrupt person even when he was in school, although he did not bother others then. Later on we found out that he had seduced the servant of a shopkeeper, Bashir, who used to sell bottles. This servant was a poor boy and was only thirteen years old. The case was presented to us and we pursued it. I met with the boy's parents but they refused to charge him. I even reprimanded them and encouraged them to come public with their allegations but they did not. I told them that keeping it a secret was not good for the market but they kept quiet. Why? Because Javed Iqbal gave them money to stay silent.

"Then we had another case in our market. I won't mention his name but Javed Iqbal did the same thing. He sexually abused a teenager. When I found out, I took the case to the local police. They summoned Javed Iqbal this time, but once again, he paid off the parents and they refused to file a charge against him. Those cases made it clear to us that he was a great blackmailer. He was quick to find out people's weaknesses and then abuse them. He used to lend people money and then exploit them.

"Once when he was sexually abusing someone we caught him and beat him up publicly with slippers. We wanted to humiliate him and teach him a lesson. We wanted to make an example out of him, so that nobody would do that again in our community. We asked him to write an apology and a promise that he would not only not do it again but also leave the market."

"Do you believe Javed Iqbal killed one hundred children?"

"He was a coward. He could never do such a thing. His criminal activities were at a very low level. I can say with great confidence and responsibility that he could not kill one hundred children. Whenever he was caught in the past he bribed people and got off the hook. He never killed anyone. His companions might have killed some people but he is not capable of murdering people."

"Do you think he was ever sexually abused himself when he was a boy?"

"When he was in the school in Ram Gali he was sexually abused. First he was abused himself and then he started abusing others. He was fond of it. He used to say, 'I am abusing others to take revenge.' I used to tell him 'You should go back to your own neighbourhood to take revenge. Don't do it in our neighbourhood. It is very embarrassing for us in this community.' Finally he promised to leave this area and went to live in Ghazi-abad.

"While he was living there he came to see me once. He showed me a magazine and bragged, 'I'm the publisher of this anti-corruption magazine.' Then he showed me his card and said, 'If ever you need any help, please let me know.' I responded, ' I can't imagine what help you could ever be to me. I can just wish you the best. I am quite happy with the grace of God.'

"Once I was sitting in the office of Shahab-ud-din, the Chief of the Shadbagh Police, when Javed Iqbal came with a friend and threw a magazine on his desk and said, 'Have a look at my magazine! I have published some nice pictures of you' He used to try to manipulate everybody, especially with his money."

"In your opinion, what happened that Javed Iqbal's marriage failed?"

"As the President of Shadbagh Business Organization and Chairman of the Conflict Resolution Council, I used to deal with many family conflicts. My colleague here, Ismail Butt, used to assist me with that. We were presented with a case that Javed Iqbal had sodomized his wife and she had refused to live with him. We pleaded with his wife to go back to him if he promised that he would not do that again. He promised, but then he tried it again and she left him for good. That was the point at which we realized that he was only interested in boys and had no sexual interest in women."

"How are things here in the market these days?" I asked the group. They came across as solid, well-meaning citizens, who had tried their best as a community to understand Javed Iqbal and at the same time confront him about his antisocial behaviour. But he pushed the limits to the point where they finally washed their hands of him and simply wanted him out of their neighborhood.

"With the grace of God, we are doing alright here, and we are free of those scandals since he left." Arif Butt's reply conveyed such a sense of relief that Javed Iqbal was long since gone from their neighborhood and no longer their problem.

After I returned from interviewing the neighbours, I again took out all the documents that Javed Iqbal's family had given me. I wanted to read the evidence of his homosexual encounters. The first document I found was the police report of 1990 when Javed Iqbal was charged for the first time and sent to jail.

POLICE REPORT 1990
Police Station, Shadbagh Lahore

Report No.	243/90
Case 12-7-79...Islamic Law:	Sodomy
Reported by:	Mohammad Iqbal son of Abdul Ghani Pathan
	House 486 Nabi Baksh Park Lahore
Witnesses:	Mohammad Aslam and Zulfiqar Pathan
Place of Incident:	Kothi 144 Near Girls College Shadbagh, Lahore
Date:	September 15th, 1990

I, Mohammad Iqbal, living at the above address and running a business in Landa Bazaar make the following statement to police.

Yesterday, on September 14th, I went to the mosque to offer my Friday prayers. When I returned home, my nine-year-old son Mohammad Irfan was not at home. I got worried. I came out and asked my brother Mohammad Aslam if he had seen Irfan. He said he saw Irfan on a bicycle with another ten-year-old boy. So I, my brother Aslam and a friend Zulfiqar (Pathan) went looking for my son. When we passed in front of Mohammad Ali and Javed Iqbal's house we heard my son Irfan crying. We pushed open the door, which was not locked from inside, and went in. We saw my son Irfan lying on the ground with his pants down and saw Javed Iqbal son of Mohammad Ali lying on top of him with his pants down performing sodomy. When Javed Iqbal heard us coming, he got up, pulled his pants up and ran away.

My son Irfan told me that when he and his friend were passing in front of that house, Javed Iqbal came out and stopped them. He sent the other boy to his aunt's house and brought my son inside. Then he took my son's pants off and asked him to lie down on the ground. Then he took his own pants off and started having sex with him. When he screamed with pain he put his hand on his mouth. In the meanwhile you people came. I am reporting that Javed Iqbal son of Mohammad Ali resident of 144 Shadbagh Lahore performed sodomy with my son Irfan.

Police Officer Nasrullah Khan

Then I started looking through the diaries that Javed Iqbal had written when he was charged. Interestingly, Javed Iqbal had a habit of keeping a record of his activities. Those diaries highlighted his state of mind. He never believed he had done anything wrong. He called it a "misunderstanding".

OLD DIARIES OF JAVED IQBAL
September 1990 — March 1991

September 14th.   There is a police case against me based on a misunderstanding. I was upset all night long. Saeed was with me. I took 10,000 rupees from him and delivered them to Moghalpura.

September 15th.   Haji, Dad and Pervaiz Sahib got arrested by the police. I went to Gujranwala for the day.

September 16th.   Met Iqbal. He brought 10,000 rupees for Mom. Left for Rawalpindi at noon. Yaseen and his son came along. We stayed in a hotel in Murree.

September 17th.   Spent the day in the hotel, mentally upset.

September 18th.   Telephoned Lahore. Stayed in the hotel in Murree.

September 19th.   Spend the day looking for a new hotel. Spent the night in the same hotel.

September 20th.   Found another place to stay. Did shopping all day long. Gave 1200 rupees as advance.

September 21st.   Spent all day long worried.

September 22nd.   Left for Lahore. At 9 p.m. called Saeed from Moghulpura. Arrived home. Slept in Ram Gali. Iqbal got arrested.

September 23rd.   Worried about Iqbal's arrest. I am feeling pressure from my family. They want me arrested. I left home in the morning but after having a meeting with Chaudhry Gul Asghar I came back home. Sold gold.

September 24th.   Some heated arguments with brother. Expression of bitterness. False promises. Went to Iqbal's house. Spent a sleepless night. I wanted to go but stayed on the request of my mom. I am worried about Iqbal.

September 26th.   Stayed in bed all day long. In the evening Saeed handed me over to the police. I spent the night in police custody. I met Iqbal in prison. I gave the SHO [Station House Officer] police officer 4000 rupees that I had in my pocket.

September 27th.   Spent the day in isolation but spent the night sleeping with Iqbal in custody.

D r .   K .   S o h a i l

September 28th.	Spent the day with Iqbal. Met Agha Sahib today. Nobody came from home to see me. I am so worried I have lost my appetite. I spent the night with Iqbal in custody.
September 29th.	I am not eating or drinking anything. SHO is giving me a hard time. I put pressure on my family. I got a message from Dad that he has offered 20,000 rupees to make a peaceful offer.
September 30th.	I was presented in front of the Superintendent of Police. Sent for medical examination. Iqbal was set free. Spent the first night alone in custody.
October 7th.	Met Ameen, Yaseen and then Saeed, Pervaiz and Haji today. Got 500 rupees from Saeed.
November 5th.	Got 1000 rupees from Yaseen. Gave the gatekeeper and staff 700 rupees and bought things for 150 rupees.
November 7th.	Got 1000 rupees from Yaseen.
November 26th.	Went to court today. I have to appear again on December 8th, 1990.
January 5th.	Went to court. Met Haji Sahib and Zia. He promised he will arrange bail in 15 days. He brought some fruit and sweets for Abid Chaudhry.
March 16th.	Session court set me free today.

It was interesting for me to read here that Javed Iqbal confesses his intimate relationship with Iqbal. He was his employee and later on became his brother-in-law.

FATHER'S LETTER TO JAVED IQBAL

Javed Iqbal's relationship with his father intrigued me. In spite of his father's embarrassment about his son's lifestyle and going to jail, he never abandoned him. He kept offering financial and emotional support. Finally it got to the point when he felt tired and exhausted and drained. He did not know how to help his son any more so he sent him the following letter in jail.

My dear son Javed Iqbal! Assalam-o-alaikum!

On your insistence I am writing this letter. We are worried about you day and night. I did not want to upset you in jail but if you want to know the truth then I will share the harsh realities with you. For you to ask fifty thousand or one lakh [100,000] rupees is no big deal, but let me tell you that your father is not a rich landlord. I do not have any fixed earning. I work from seven in the morning to seven at night to earn my honest living. Whatever I earned I improved my business or spent on the weddings of my children. I spent my life with dignity with the grace of God. Because of your activities and going to jail we have faced embarrassment and humiliation in the community. I spent a lot of money to help you but I was not successful. Now I am too embarrassed to ask for any more loan and nobody would give me any more even if I dared to ask. The only thing left is my car. I can sell it anytime but I need it.

I was a part of four one-lakh rupe - committees and I have to make regular payments. I have already paid 1600 rupees in the first, 9000 in the second, 4000 in the third and 30,000 in the fourth committee.

Yaseen Sahib has also been involved in committees and comes every few days to get 100 rupees. In the past whatever you asked I gave it to you. But now I am reaching my limit. Nasim came to discuss your case with me. I promised to help him. Haji Ejaz is also trying to help you. All I can reassure is that I am trying my best and I will keep on trying to help you. I am not unaware of your predicament.

Wassalam, Mohhammad Ali

Javed Iqbal was charged with sodomy a second time in 1998. He believed he had been framed by his friends who owed him money. Pervez Iqbal, his brother, also believed that. It is apparent that Javed Iqbal was losing support from his friends, and after his father's death, also from his family. I found the police report from that charge.

POLICE REPORT
FEBRUARY 1998

Reported by:	Faqir Mohammad son of Fateh Mohammad at the Police Station, Lower Mall Lahore
Crime: 12-7-79	Islamic Law...Sodomy
Place of Incident:	Main Bazaar Data Darbar
Reported on:	February 12th, 98
Police Officer:	Nadeem Yaseen

I, Faqeer Mohammad, who live in the Lower Mall Lahore and work in Machli Mandi for the last 40 years, father of 11 sons and 5 daughters report the following happenings to police.

My two sons Yaser Abbas, age nine years, and Qamar Abbas, age 11 years, live with me in Machli Mandi and work in a shop with Riaz who runs a stationary store. On 9th of February 1998, I went to the village for some important work. When I returned today from the village my sons Yaser Abbas and Qamar Abbas, while crying, told me that on the 9th of February both of them went to the shrine of Data Darbar to offer prayers. At about 9:30 a.m., a man (later on we found he was Javed Iqbal, son of Mohammad Ali resident of 144 Shadbagh) got us in his car and asked us to help him look for his son. He drove around for a while and then took us to a dark alley. He took out his pistol and asked us to take off our clothes. We were so scared we got undressed. Then he took off his own clothes and had sodomy with us. Then he gave us 113 rupees and threw us out of the car. Then he asked us to come back to Data Darbar on Thursday and wait for him.'

So I with Abdul Lateef and my two sons went back to Data Darbar. We waited for him. Javed Iqbal came in his car (Plate No. 905 LHU). As soon as the car stopped we got hold of Javed Iqbal and his car and now we are handing him and the car over to the police.

I am reporting that Javed Iqbal performed sodomy with my sons.

Reading those police reports, I became curious about Pakistani laws dealing with homosexuality. I was curious whether the crime of sodomy applied only to sex with minors or included any sexual activity between two consenting adults of the same sex. So I called Mr. Minto and asked, "According to Pakistani law is there any difference between homosexual encounters between two adults and an adult and a child?"

He told me, "No, there is no difference whatsoever. The perpetrator of a crime of sodomy, whether he commits it with an adult or a child is equally guilty. So there is no distinction on that account at all."

JAVED IQBAL'S LETTER TO THE POLICE AND MEDIA

On the 17th of September, 1998, I and my 12-year-old employee Arbab were brutally killed. Arbab was hit on his head with the butt of a gun and I had multiple fractures of head and backbone. I was unconscious for twenty-two days in a general hospital. The doctors had given up on me. They thought I would die. When I regained consciousness, I was a disabled man. Without any rehabilitation they sent me home from the hospital.

I and young Arbab were beaten up by my two employees while we were asleep. One of them escaped while the other one was caught and handed over to the police. They also stole my 8000 rupees. The police officer of Ghazi-abad, rather than charging the criminal, kept him in his house as a servant. I was enraged by the cruel behaviour of my employees and the unfair role of police. I discussed the whole case with my friends and made a plan to take revenge. My childhood friend Murshad Naseem was great help in putting the plan into action. We decided that we would kill one hundred teenagers who run away from home, gather at Minar-e-Pakistan, steal people's belongings and get involved in homosexual relationships. We wanted to take revenge by getting rid of them. By killing them I wanted to take revenge on people who wanted to kill me.

Murshad planned to get 16 cans and 3 plastic drums and fill them with Sulphuric acid, Hydrochloric acid and Cyanide. The first murder was of Yasir, a 14 year-old boy from Hafizabad. We put a mask on his face full of acid and cyanide. He died within seconds. We put his dead body in the drum full of 70 kilos of acid that we had bought for 140 rupees. The acid dissolved the dead body in one day and we flushed the whole thing in a gutter. Our experiment of killing a teenager was a great success. After that we kept on bringing young boys, killing them and dissolving the dead bodies in acid. Since these boys had run away from home, nobody knew about their disappearance. This bloodbath went on for 6 months. My friends fully cooperated with me in this project. Although I had started this killing project as revenge, for my friends it had become recreational, some did it for fun, some to make money and some to sexually abuse teenagers. I had become disabled. I was losing my eyesight. I could hardly walk without support. In spite of many operations I still could not keep my balance. Sometimes when I walked, I was afraid of falling down. I had also lost my mental balance. At times I used to feel giddy and disoriented. I was so close to death. This was all because of my two employees, that I had hired from Yadgar-e-Pakistan, who had tried to kill me. One was from Kohat and the other from Narowaal. They had run away from home. To take revenge on them I killed a hundred other boys living a similar lifestyle.

I had prayed to be able to kill one hundred children and God helped me in completing my project, my promise to myself and God. The day I completed my project I thanked God for listening to my prayers. God helped me in taking my revenge. He gave me the courage and my friends the dedication to finish what we had started. It was all to teach employees a lesson so that they are never cruel with their employers.

I saw my mother sitting next to my bed crying and giving sacrifices for my recovery. But I could not recover. I could not work. I became a living corpse. My mother was so affected that she had a heart attack and died. After her death I decided to take revenge on other mothers and make them suffer the way my employees made my mother suffer by trying to kill me.

The Myth of the Chosen One

Now that I have succeeded in my master plan to kill one hundred children, I cannot wait to share the news with the rest of the world. I cannot keep it a secret any more.

I am sending you the names and addresses and dates of killings of all the children and pictures of 57 of them in this letter. When the DIG [Deputy Inspector General (Police)] of police is ready I also want to hand over 32 pages of my diary which has all the details of the murders. I am also planning to hand myself over to the police, as I am not afraid of death anymore. I am contemplating pleading guilty on behalf of my friends and getting the punishment because I had asked them to act on my master plan. I hope that I succeed in my plan with the grace of God. Amen

Wassalam, Javed Iqbal

⌛ 11 *A Prolonged Nightmare*

The contents of the letter to the police hinted at some confusing motives and rationalizations for the grandiose murder plan. I wanted to look into the circumstances related to Javed Iqbal's hospitalization and its relationship to the murders. So I contacted Pervez Iqbal, the older brother, as I had found him quite open and psychologically sophisticated. He was willing to meet with me again.

This time we were alone, and he seemed more relaxed with me, realizing that I was truly interested in understanding his troubled brother, and not just there to get a sensational story.

A child brought us each a glass of juice and Pervez took a few moments to collect his thoughts.

"One day I was working on the second floor of this building, when I saw some people stop their car in front and get out. They called me and asked me to come down. I did not feel comfortable the way they talked to me. I was suspicious. They were in plain clothes, not in any uniform, but I had the feeling that they were police. Reluctantly I came down to the balcony of the first floor.

"Do you recognize this car?" they asked.

"No," I replied.

"How is Javed Iqbal related to you?" Hearing that question I felt a cold shudder. I had flashbacks to the 1990 case and the one of 1997. Is this the third episode? I asked myself. I was nervous but I went downstairs.

"'What kind of brother are you?' they said. 'You do not recognize your brother's car.' When I reassured them that I was telling the truth they told me that it was Javed's car and someone had shot him. I did not believe them. I knew that if Javed were in his right frame of mind nobody could kill him. Those people wanted me to go with them to get his belongings as he was in hospital but I refused. Some other neighbours came to support me. When I made it clear that I would not go and claim Javed's belongings, they said they would keep them in the police station. With their rude attitude I had a strong suspicion that they were police officers in plain clothes.

"An hour later, my younger brother Saeed came with Javed's servant Yaseen and confirmed that Javed was on his deathbed in the hospital. When I heard that news I decided to go the hospital with my brother. When I entered the hospital I saw the police there and also the men who had come to see me in my house. When they saw me they said, 'Here he comes. He is Javed Iqbal's brother. Arrest him.' When I heard that I got scared. I was soaked in sweat from head to toe. I remembered being in police custody in 1990. They grabbed me and dragged me aside. They wanted to investigate me. Because of the legal disputes they were suspicious of all of us brothers. They thought one of us might have tried to kill him. When we heard that, we panicked. I told them I had come to see my brother who was dying and we should deal with legal matters later on. They let me go. I searched all over the ward but could not find my brother. When the doctor pointed towards the bed I realized that he had been so badly beaten up that I could not recognize him. His face was all swollen and he was just wearing a tee shirt and underwear. He was hardly breathing. There were tubes full of blood coming out everywhere. Looking at him I felt giddy. The doctor saw my condition and sent me out of the ward. He suggested I not come back in, and he also told me that Javed Iqbal was probably going to die soon. He said only a miracle could save him and even if he survived he might not be mentally fit afterwards.

"Outside the ward we met with the police and told them we would come to the police station in the evening. They let us go. At night we went to report to the police station. They forced us to file a case although we had not witnessed anything. We did not want to get into trouble and be accused of murder so we filed a case. We told them we had no intentions of pursuing the case, as we were just fulfilling the formalities. After that we came home.

"Three weeks later Javed Iqbal regained consciousness. During that attack on him, a twelve-year-old young boy had also been hurt. He had been admitted to the Mayo Hospital. We used to go to both hospitals although they were quite far away from each other, hoping that both Javed and the boy would live. We were also hoping that once the boy regained consciousness, he could tell the police that we were innocent.

"Although Javed Iqbal and the boy regained consciousness, they could not tell what had happened. Both had received head injuries. Javed Iqbal had multiple fractures of his skull and jaw. When the general hospital discharged him, we took him to the dental hospital but they did not give him proper attention. They ignored us and treated us like animals. It was suggested we see a doctor privately. He told us it would cost us 96000 Rupees for the initial work-up and then more for the operations. We could not afford that much money.

"Then we were advised to go to the Services Hospital where we saw Doctor Kashif. He was very kind and sympathetic. He admitted Javed and talked to the staff in the Dental Surgery Department about operating on him. They operated on his jaw but not on his skull. To pay for his operations, Javed Iqbal had to sell his house.

"In the meanwhile, the young boy had him charged, which we found odd, since in our presence he had never mentioned any sexual abuse. To deal with that charge, Javed had to pay the boy's father some money. Since Javed did not have that much money left, my mom had to provide the money for that payment.

"During that time we met Iqbal, Javed's servant who was very close to him. They had grown up together. When Mom told him what had happened to Javed, he came along and looked after him. At that time Mom was not feeling well herself. She had heart problems. My younger sister was recently divorced at that time, and Mom was worried about getting her married again. Mom lived in her house with her for a while. Mom was quite impressed by how Iqbal looked after Javed during his convalescence, so she thought he might make a good husband for her daughter. Mom discussed this proposal with us and asked us to go to Ravi Road to discuss it with Javed Iqbal.

"That was the only time I saw his house on Ravi Road. It was a strange house. There was a verandah in the front and then a long room. Then there was a second room inside the first and then a third inside the second room. I did not see any big gutter. The house is a cup-shaped and people living in other houses can see inside. If someone screamed there, the neighbours would have easily heard the noise. I cannot believe that a hundred children were killed there."

We discussed the logistics of the murders and the house layout for awhile, but we kept coming back to Javed Iqbal's lifestyle and character. He was an unusual man with a well-known unconventional lifestyle, but was he a serial killer? I thanked Pervez for his input and returned home to pore over the documents.

The more I thought about the case, the more I started to doubt the whole story of the murders of a hundred children. Reading Javed Iqbal's diaries again, I began to have doubts about the story. It seemed that facts and fiction, fantasies and realities were all mixed together. I started to wonder whether Javed Iqbal was confabulating as he had received severe brain damage after being in a coma for twenty-two days.

My first clue was when I read in his diaries "...my daughter and wife Nazli came to see me this evening and brought lots of flowers," while the police investigations had noted that his wife and daughter had not seem him for years.

My second clue was when I read the following statement in the judge's verdict where he quotes the defense lawyer:

"(It is an admitted fact that the present case is totally based on circumstantial evidence and there exists no direct evidence in this case.) The learned defense counsel while arguing on this *point categorically submitted that in the absence of any direct evidence, no person can be convicted. It is next argued that no person can be convicted in the absence of direct medical evidence; where there is no dead body available and no actual cause of death can be determined. No allegation regarding the killing of any human being can be leveled against any of the accused person. Learned defense counsel further argued that the prosecution has failed to produce any direct evidence in this case regarding the commission of any offence, and circumstantial evidence on which the prosecution is trying to base their case is no help to it."*

My third clue was when I read in a local magazine *"GHAZI"* of January 4th, 2000, that three of the hundred missing children had safely returned home.

Finally I decided to pick one incident from Javed Iqbal's diaries which I could test with my limited resources. I was quite aware that I was not a police investigator, but as a mental health professional, I wanted to explore the matter. So when I read the following entry in the diary of November 22nd, I remembered that when I first met Javed Iqbal's family, I had met the nephew Waseem who is mentioned here. The entry in the diary reads:

"November 6th. Today all three of my nephews (Waseem Pervaiz, Shahbaz Aijaz and Nomi Jabbar) came at 5pm. They brought a beautiful 16 year-old girl with them. The girl was very upset. Waseem took me aside and told me, 'Uncle! We are in big trouble. Please help us!' When I asked the details, he said, 'This girl is a friend of a girl who works in our house as a servant. She ran away from her village. She stayed at our place for a while. I seduced her. Then I introduced her to Nomi and Shahbaz. We all slept with her. Then she left. Now she has come back after three months and told us that she is pregnant. She wants us to do something, otherwise, her parents will take us to court. She is asking me to marry her. We brought her here so that you can help. We know that you are helping people get

rid of their enemies. Please get rid of this girl.' Sajid told me that Shahzad overheard our conversation and told him that we were going to get rid of that girl. I asked Waseem to take the chain and put it around the girl's neck from the back while I kept her busy talking. We closed the door. When Waseem acted on my suggestion, the girl struggled but Shahbaz, Nomi and I held onto her. We turned up the volume on the TV and choked her.

"I told the boys that I also wanted to get rid of Shahzad. Waseem put the chain around his neck too, and we all helped him in killing Shahzad. Then we put both dead bodies in the drums and asked my three nephews to pour in the acid. Because of them I could not take pictures of the girl and Shahzad, neither did I ask the girl for her address. All three boys were very happy they succeeded in the project. I told them to keep it a secret. They promised they would not tell anyone and left."

I felt that Waseem, who had not been charged with anything and who was living at home with his family, would provide significant testimony about the case, testimony that was not available from any other source. When I called the family to request a meeting with him, he was kind enough to agree to a meeting that afternoon.

When I arrived at the house, Waseem came to the door himself, and showed me in. He was a dapper young man, very self-possessed and personable. He shared with me that he had always wanted to be an actor. He had heard that I had produced a number of documentaries and was keen to find out if I could connect him with some film people. We chatted about directors and movies for awhile and then I steered him towards a discussion of his experiences with the police. He was quite open about what had happened.

"One day, as I was doing some work at home here, I heard some children shouting out in the street, 'The police are here!' I said to my mother, 'So what?' and went on reading my book. But the police car stopped in front of our house here. I went outside to have a look and one of the officers asked me, 'Who are you?' I said, 'Waseem.' Then he went back to the car. After a while they came back and asked me to get into the police car with them. In the meanwhile, my mom came downstairs and asked the officer, 'Where are you taking my son?'

"Then I got really nervous. I asked them, 'Where are you taking me?' They said, 'We have to interrogate you about a case.'

"I asked, 'What kind of a case?' because I knew nothing. They took me to the police station at Ravi Road. The officer held me by the collar and dragged me in. Then two inspectors beat me up. They treated me as if I were a criminal. In reality the real criminal, Javed Iqbal, was missing. Then two officers, Pervaiz Qandhari and Tariq Mehmood came and had a meeting and put me in a jeep.

"They took me to the police station of Qilla Gujar Singh. I was asked to go into the Inspector's office.

"'He asked me, 'What is your name?'

"I said, 'Waseem.'

"'He asked, 'How are you related to Javed Iqbal?'

"I said, 'He is my uncle.'

"We had heard as children that our Uncle Javed Iqbal got into trouble in the past and my father and grandfather had to go to the police station. I thought he had done some other mischief.

"Then the Inspector invited a constable in and asked him to interrogate me. He took me to another room and told me that Javed Iqbal had mentioned in his diaries that I had killed a girl. Can you believe it, Doctor! He had also mentioned my two other cousins, Shahbaz and Nadeem. The Constable told me that I, Shahbaz and Nadeem had taken a girl to my other uncle's place and that we had sex with her and when we found out that she was pregnant, we killed her.

"'What am I accused of?' I asked the constable.

"That you have killed a girl," he answered.

"The constable hit me with a stick and then took me back into the Inspector's office. In the meanwhile Tariq Camboh came. He saw me crying and took me to another room where my father and two uncles were present. He left me with them and went away.

"The police were looking for Javed Iqbal and they had arrested us instead. We were worried all night long and then the next day. They interrogated us many times one by one. At night-time they put shackles on our feet. It was very painful. We suffered a lot."

I had my answer, at least to that part of the mystery. We chatted for a while longer about Waseem's acting ambitions, and I was satisfied that he was what he seemed to be, a bright, well-adjusted young man who had been yet another victim of his Uncle Javed Iqbal's bizarre agenda.

While I was interviewing Waseem it dawned on me that the whole case of Javed Iqbal had created a living nightmare for the family. They were very generous to share the story but also wanted to highlight that they were decent people and belonged to a respectable family. They were not a family of sinners and criminals, rather they were respectable citizens and had many members who were very holy.

While I was there, Javed Iqbal's younger brother Saeed came in and joined us, so I had the opportunity to talk to him as well. He was quite open about the situation.

"We did not see him that often when I was young as he didn't live around here and he had his own life. I was not very attached to him. I know that he used to do a lot of volunteer work and he was very active in the Market Association. Then he got involved with video games and sports but he was always found with boys. He had also started a school for children, called Sunnyside School. It was in Shadbagh and it was the first air-conditioned school in this area."

"How did you feel when Javed Iqbal's case became public?"

"What could we feel? It was tragic. We never believed he could do something like that. We found out more through newspapers since, as I said, we rarely saw him."

Saeed glanced at Waseem. "You know, he came once to see me. He told me about this plan he had, but I didn't believe him. He told me that he had found a formula to end the world. There was no mention of the boys. I told him, life and death are in God's hands. In the morning he went back home and then I never saw him again."

"What did you think of his mental state at that time?"

"I thought that since he had received many head injuries and skull fractures, he must have lost his mind. I thought he had become mentally paralyzed."

"How was his physical health?"

"At times he looked fine, at other times he needed to lean on one of the boys' shoulder to walk. If people speculated as to why there were always boys with him, he used to say, 'I need them for support.'

"Mom died on July 26th, 1999. During the sixteen days she was in the hospital, he came to visit her every day. He would come at night and stayed there for hours, sometimes till two or three a.m. but not in her room, he stayed outside. After her death, we seldom saw him any more. Then suddenly, his name was on everybody's lips throughout the whole country."

"How did this crisis affect your family?"

He grimaced and shook his head. "Doctor, we are living in hell. We have lost respect in everybody's eyes and our children's future is ruined. The schools are refusing to enroll our children. Now what is our fault in this case? We are all paying for his deeds. We are being punished for his actions. Some people are sympathetic and realize we are innocent but others judge us harshly and are cruel. Except for him, we are all law-abiding citizens. We have such a family atmosphere that nobody even curses in our family."

"What kind of personality does he have?"

"He is very intelligent and very determined. He succeeds in convincing others of whatever he wants even if he is wrong. He is a great liar. He exaggerates things. Even now his stories are ninety-nine per cent lies."

On that note of disgust, we parted.

The interesting thing was that on one hand Javed Iqbal had written confessions and sent detailed letters to the police and media but in court he had recanted. I was curious about his motivation for changing the story. So I decided to go back to see him to put those questions to him.

This time, there was no problem getting in to see him. The Superintendent of the jail was very helpful in arranging for the second interview. But when I was escorted by the guards to Javed Iqbal's cell, he looked subdued. He welcomed me but not as enthusiastically as before. He put down his tasbeeh and sat watching me silently.

After some inquiries about his health, which he brushed off impatiently, I got right to my point. "After you went to the papers with your confession you disappeared. The police could not find you for a month. Where were you hiding?"

"I was in the jungle for four weeks. The police kept on looking for me but could not find me. Finally I decided to hand myself and my friends over and I went to the newspaper office. I had even contemplated suicide. I went to Ravi River and wanted to drown myself but then I did not. I thought if I died, who would tell my story? I want the whole world to know my story and the story of hundreds of children who are abused and killed every day in Pakistan. I know all the people including police officers who are involved."

"Now tell me honestly, Javed Iqbal, did you kill one hundred children?"

He looked straight into my eyes and said, "Do you think a man who has been disabled, who can hardly walk, who has difficulties going to the washroom, is strong enough to kill one hundred children?"

"Did you sexually abuse children?"

"I love children. I made a special air-conditioned school, called Sunnyside School, for them. I set up video-centers for them. I wanted to rescue them from all the abuse they suffer in our corrupt system. I have been wrongly accused all my life." He was quite defensive.

"If you did not kill or abuse children, then why did your disciples also confess to those killings?"

"You must have read what happened to my companion Ishaq Billa. If you have not read the articles, please do. The police, while investigating the case, killed him, as they realized that he was one of the key witnesses. So to protect my other friends, I told them to say 'yes' to everything the police asked them. It was to save their lives. All those confessions are fake. They have no value. They are not true."

"If you did not do these killings, then why did you go to the newspaper office and give them this false story?"

"Dr. Sohail! After living in this country all my life and being part of a corrupt system, I came to the realization that the system can change only from the outside. Only when this corruption comes under the scrutiny of international interrogation and investigation, only then there is some hope of its reform. So to get international attention, I had to orchestrate this big drama. And that is why I am giving you all the details hoping that you will narrate my story and the story of this corrupt society to the whole world. They can kill me. But if the environment and circumstances do not change, there will be another Javed Iqbal."

He turned back to his tasbeeh to signify the end of the interview. I would have liked to ask him more but clearly he had had enough. I thanked him once again and called the guards to escort me out.

My mind was a discordant whirl of thoughts and issues.

⧗ 12 The police and the Crime

After talking to Javed Iqbal this time, I focused on the case of Ishaq Billa and the role of the police. What I discovered in the newspaper articles was unbelievable. On December 2nd 1999, when Javed Iqbal disappeared, the police all over the country started looking for his gang, one member of which was Ishaq Billa. When they could not find him, they arrested his father, the way they had arrested Javed Iqbal's father in the past. On December 6th, 1999, Ishaq Billa's mother took him to the police station and handed him over, to secure the release of her husband. On December 8th, it was reported that Ishaq Billa had jumped from the second floor of the police station and committed suicide. Ishaq Billa's family was distraught and highly suspicious of that report.

While I was reading Khizr Hayat Gondal"s book *Sau Bachol ka Qatl* [Murder of Hundred Children] I found the following statement:

> *"In the first week of December 1999, Ishaq Billa died in police custody. The police reported that during the investigation Ishaq Billa jumped from the second story and killed himself. DSP [District Superintendant of Police] Tariq Camboh claimed that because of the fear of the case becoming public, he committed suicide.*
>
> *Ishaq Billa's relatives strongly feel that he was abused and killed by the police and then thrown out of the window. Ishaq Billa was handed over to the police by his mother on*

December 6th, 1999, as his father was being kept in police cus-
tody in exchange for the arrest of the son. Ishaq Billa died on
December 8th, 1999.

Chief Secretary Punjab Hafeez Akhtar made a statement
that it could not be ruled out that to protect other police officers,
the police had killed a key witness in Javed Iqbal's case. He
shared that DSP Tariq Camboh, ASI Shahid Mahmood and
another police officer have been arrested as Ishaq Billa was in
their custody when he died. Governor Punjab expressed his
anger and considered it a case of police negligence. He wanted
it to be investigated further."

The postmortem report showed that Ishaq Billa died of
head injuries. The medical board said that he had eggshell frac-
tures of his skull. They also found signs of violence on his body.
His face and shoulders were bruised and swollen. He had sev-
enteen wounds out of which nine were one to three days old.
Ishaq Billa's postmortem was supervised by a team of seven
doctors."

As I carefully read the judge's verdict, I realized that even the
judge had felt that the police had submitted false evidence regarding
the bones found in the drums recovered from Javed Iqbal's house. He
had written:

"...these bones which are not found to be of human origin, are
in fact the over-zealous doing of the police and I think this is a
sheer plantation by the Police Officer because there was the
Investigating Officer of this case, and when the Investigating
officer was available in Lahore, what was the fun in sending a
Police Officer, who was not the Investigating Officer by only a
telephonic message to the place of occurrence which as per the
persecution case, was sealed at that time ... I also depreciate
this practice of the police whereby they tried to show extra effi-
ciency."

The judge also realized that police officers were grossly negligent in not taking the complaints of parents seriously. He wrote:

"Here I also want to express my opinion regarding the irresponsibility and indifferent attitude of police who miserably failed to search even a single boy who left his house on some pretext and rather they put such a cold shoulder and avoided their liabilities in such a manner that even legal heir appearing before me complained of the fact that they approached the police for registration of FIR [First Investigation Report] regarding the missing of their child but the police refused to do so. This is an alarming situation and I would write separately in this regard to the concerned authorities."

It is no surprise then that when Ishaq Billa's case was investigated further, the police officers in charge of the case were in serious trouble. Khizr Hayat wrote:

"The Punjab Government has charged DSP Tariq Camboh, SPC Pervaiz Qandhari, SHO Imtiaz Bhalli and ASI Shahid Murad for murdering Ishaq Billa while he was in police custody. The case has been forwarded for judicial inquiry."

⌛ 13 *Major and Minor Criminals*

While I was studying the judge's verdict once again, I called Mr. Minto one evening and asked him, "The other three boys who have been convicted alongside Javed Iqbal are teenagers. The medical reports say they have reached puberty physically but they are not eighteen years old. One of them will be hanged alongside Javed Iqbal. How does Pakistani law determine who is a minor and who is an adult?"

He said, "In the penal code there is a different conception of a person who is capable of committing an offence as compared to the general law of majority. The general law of majority in Pakistan is that a male of eighteen years becomes an adult but that is for purposes of various other activities, for example transactions that he undertakes.

"But as far as penal law is concerned, the penal code itself provides that if a person is seven or less than seven years of age he is supposed to have committed no offence. So a child of seven years or below cannot be convicted of an offence under the penal code. A child between twelve and seventeen can be convicted of an offense which he commits provided he is mature enough to understand the consequences of the act that he commits. It is not the question of puberty. It is the maturity of the mind which will determine from the various circumstances and from asking questions of the accused himself that he is a mature person. And if the judge is convinced that he is a mature person, he can give him the punishment which is provided by the law. But invariably in such circumstances the maximum punishment is not awarded because of the age itself. And that is the law as far as the penal law of Pakistan is concerned."

"A couple of times Javed Iqbal mentioned that he wanted to commit suicide, although he never did. How is attempted suicide seen in the eyes of the law?"

"Well, Dr. Sohail, this is a criminal offence under the penal code of Pakistan. Anyone who attempts suicide will be charged with that offence and will be sentenced."

⌛ 14 *Saints and Sinners*

On an afternoon when Shoaib had some free time, we went to visit the shrine of Data Ganj Baksh. Thousands of people there were there having their *langar* [the soup kitchen of Pakistan]. I shared with Shoaib that whenever my mother had to pray for something special she sacrificed two black lambs and sent them to the holy shrine to feed the poor and needy. During my visit I wondered how Javed Iqbal could come here and pray and while praying, meditate about abusing and killing one hundred children.

After visiting the shrine, we went to see the Badshahi mosque. It looked as graceful as ever. Shoaib took me to see the museum and I was amazed to see the rare religious items collected from all over the world. In front of the mosque was the Lahore Fort, in which emperors of the Moghul Dynasty, who ruled India for seven generations, had made many architectural changes over the centuries. Shoaib told me that of all the Moghul kings, he was most fascinated with Jahangir especially his relationship with his wife Queen Noor Jehan.

"Have you heard the story of how Noor Jehan outsmarted Jahangir?" I asked him.

"No, tell me."

"Jahangir and Noor Jehan used to go for an afternoon walk once a week. One day when they came out of their palace, they started walking towards a hill. When they reached the top, they saw a village woman lying on the ground in the valley.

"'Look at that woman!' Jahangir said to Noor Jehan. As they watched from the distance, the woman gave birth to a baby, cut the umbilical with two rocks, picked up the baby and went on with her journey.

"Jahangir said sarcastically, 'How come she could do that but when you are pregnant, you need to be pampered for months before and after the delivery?' Noor Jehan, a wise woman, kept quiet.

The next day Noor Jehan called the Head Gardener and asked him not to water the plants for a week. He said, 'Your Highness! Do you realize what you are asking? We have special flowers from all over the world in our garden. If we don't water them, they will die.' When Noor Jehan insisted, he left, puzzled.

"The next week when Noor Jehan and Jahangir went for a walk, Jahangir was shocked to see most of his favourite roses dead in the garden. Enraged, Jahangir summoned the Head Gardener. Noor Jehan was watching it all quietly. When the Head Gardener came, Jahangir demanded, 'Why did you not water the plants?' The poor man replied respectfully, 'Your Excellency! It was ordered by Her Highness.' Jahangir looked at Noor Jehan who only smiled. He let the Head Gardener go and asked Noor Jehan, 'Why the hell did you order that?'

"'Don't get upset. Look at the hill. You see thousands of wild trees. Who waters them?'

"It took Jahangir a few seconds to realize that it was a response to his sarcastic remark about the village woman. He realized that the village woman was a wild tree while his queen was a delicate flower that needed to be pampered."

While talking, we reached the Minar-e-Pakistan and sat down to have snacks and drinks. I imagined that we were sitting at the place where Javed Iqbal was supposed to be hanged publicly. During our chat I asked Shoaib, "You have lived in Lahore all your life and you visit these areas frequently. There must be dozens of stories about the Badshahi mosque and Red Light Area. Share with me the most fascinating.

"Have you heard the story of Faqir Budhan Sain?"

"No, I haven't."

"There are many versions. I will tell you the version I know. Faqir Budhan Sain was a mysterious personality. He lived in one of the rooms in the Red Light Area. Everybody believed he was a saint. The police and the prostitutes respected him equally. He rarely talked, but whenever he talked everybody listened. If he did not come out of his room for a couple of days, everybody got worried. Everybody wanted his blessings. Once a local shopkeeper shouted at Sain publicly, and the next day he fell and died. People believe he was cursed for insulting Sain.

"The interesting part is that nobody knew who he was, where he was born and raised. And then in the 1950's he became the focus of public attention when a young woman by the name of Sardar Begum claimed in the local court that she was the daughter of Sain who was married to her mother Iqbal Begum in the 1920's. At that time people found out that Sain was from a very wealthy Hindu family. But in his youth he had been so impressed by Muslim mystic poetry that he became a Muslim. His Hindu family was quite upset. And when he married a Muslim woman his family disowned him. In 1947 Sain's Hindu family went to India and then he never heard from them.

"While Sardar Begum was trying to obtain her inheritance, the story took an interesting turn when another woman by the name of Hafiza Begum from the Red Light Area appeared in court and challenged Iqbal Begum. Hafiza Begum told the judge that she was married to Sain and had a son by the name of Ahmed Shuja from him. There was a major fight between the two women. Each accused the other of being a liar and manipulating Sain, while the judge listened to it quietly.

"To prove her point Sardar Begum even shared with the judge that Sain had appeared in the court with his wife in the 1920's as a witness. At that time Sain was charged with insulting an income tax officer. Sain had slapped the officer when he came to investigate his property. In the court Iqbal Begum was wearing a veil and nobody could see her face. The judge asked her to take the veil off so that the court could recognize the witness. Sain told his wife not to listen to the judge, rather to listen to her husband. Sain believed that being a dedicated Muslim nobody had the right to see his wife's face. When judge insisted Sain got so infuriated that he went forward and slapped the judge. The judge charged him with contempt of court and ordered three years imprisonment. The jail sentence changed his life. When he came out his wife was dead. He was so touched that he started writing mystic poetry himself. Not knowing his real name, people gave him a new identity and started calling him Sain and he started living in the Red Light Area. He never went back to his village. The daughter tried her best to convince the judge that she was the rightful heir, but the judge was not convinced. She even brought the register from the Badshahi Mosque to prove when her father had accepted Islam but the judge found the whole evidence inconclusive. The judge even invited Sain to court but he did not come. The judge refused to give any verdict."

"That is a fascinating story."

"Sohail! Which is the most intriguing story you have come across in your professional life?"

"The one that comes to my mind at this time is of a man in Ontario, Canada who had a commune in Lindsay. He had nine wives and twenty-seven children. The way I found out about him was that one afternoon the mother of one of my patients came to see me. She told me that she was worried her daughter was seeing an evil man. When I asked about the man, she told me that Rock Theriault was a French Canadian man who had moved to Lindsay from Quebec and had established a commune. He believed he was a holy man, but everybody else saw him as a devil. Since he did not send his children to the local school, the Children's Aid Society [CAS] gave them an ultimatum. They ordered Theriault and his wives to send the children to school or they would take them away and put them in foster homes so that they would receive a proper education. The interesting thing was that the mothers of those children were so brainwashed by Theriault that they listened to him and refused to cooperate with the CAS. Finally, the CAS took the children away and put them in foster homes.

"The CAS did not realize that they had opened a Pandora's Box. Theriault went to court and asked for his fatherly rights. The judge allowed him to visit his children every week. So when Theriault came to town to see his children, he started seducing the foster mothers. During one of his visits to town he had met my patient in a local store. Her mother was very worried, as she did not want her daughter to become his tenth wife.

"When I talked to my patient, who was a naïve gullible woman, she told me that Theriault always treated her nicely. He gave her more attention and love than she had ever received in her life. She was willing to see him in spite of her mother's disapproval. I told her mother that there was not much she could do.

"Soon after that incident, Theriault was arrested and sent to the Kingston Penitentiary. He had tried to castrate one of the men on the commune and was abusive towards some of the women.

"Although Theriault has been in jail for a number of years and will stay for another few years, some of his wives have opened a bakery in Kingston and are faithfully waiting for the day when he will be released and they will resume their communal lifestyle. When I was reading Javed Iqbal's diaries, I wondered whether these men had something in common. Both could brainwash naïve and vulnerable minds. Recently two journalists, Paul Kailla and Ross Laver, wrote a book, *Savage Messiah*, focusing on Theriault's life."

It was getting late when Shoaib and I headed home. As we were leaving we saw a number of homeless children and teenagers looking for work. I worried about the future of those children. On the way home I thanked Shoaib for being such a tremendous help during my trip. He asked me to send him a copy of my book when it was published.

FORENSIC

One of the things that intrigued me about Javed Iqbal's case was how was it possible to kill one hundred human beings in a small house in a busy congested area. Javed Iqbal's brother Pervez Iqbal believed it was not possible. He believed that if someone had screamed even once, the neighbours would have known. It was also incomprehensible to me that someone could purchase enough acid to dissolve a hundred bodies and then dispose of that acid and dissolved bodies without anyone noticing it.

I read the following Forensic Report in Khizr Hayat's book, *Sau Bachon Ka Qatl*, which answered some of my questions.

"A Forensic Scientist and the in-charge of the Forensic Science Laboratory Dr. Amir Ali Hussain expressed his concern regarding police neglect of the case of Ravi Road involving death of one hundred children. He said to dissolve one adult we need thirty gallons of acid and to dissolve a teenager's dead body we need twenty gallons of acid. He said to dissolve a hundred dead bodies, we need two to three thousand gallons. Such a large amount of acid is available only for industrial use and a strict record is kept of that much acid.

He said such an amount would cost 6 lakh [600,000] rupees. He was disappointed that the Police Department did not consult them in due time, otherwise they would have tested the sewer system and helped the police. He said if such a large amount of acid was poured in gutter, it could have been an environmental hazard causing poisonous fumes and possible fire. He did not find any scientific evidence of a spill of such a large amount of acid in Javed Iqbal's house."

REHABILITATION CONSULTANT

When I returned to Canada, I consulted Dr. Tahir Qazi, a rehabilitation consultant, to get his opinion about the possibility of Javed Iqbal having brain damage after being in a coma for twenty-two days.

Dear Dr. Tahir Qazi,

During my interviews with Javed Iqbal Mughal and his brother Pervez Iqbal, I discovered that Javed Iqbal was in the hospital in a coma for twenty-two days after he was severely beaten up by his enemies one night while he was sleeping. When I met him in the prison, he asked me to touch his forehead and face and I could feel the fractures with my fingers.

After reading his diaries I strongly feel that reality is mixed with lies and confabulations. I suspect that the brain injury caused some neurological, psychiatric and behavioral abnormalities. Since you are a rehabilitation specialist and deal with patients suffering from Traumatic Brain Injury, I would like your opinion about this case.

I strongly feel that he should have had a neuro-psychiatric evaluation prior to sentencing.

Sincerely,
Sohail

Doctor Qazi's reply was not long in coming.

Dear Dr. Sohail,

Thank you for asking my opinion. On the basis of available data, I note that Javed Iqbal Mughal was severely beaten up at one time and that he was in coma for twenty-two days and there were possible skull fractures as well. I am making this deduction on the basis of your description that there were dents in the continuity of his skull bones. Taking this information at face value would mean that we need to look at the whole picture from a medical vantage point.

If Javed Iqbal was in a coma for this long period of time, it would constitute a "Severe Traumatic Brain Injury (TBI)." From my own experience treating brain injury patients there are numerous changes in their psychosocial personality.

I would like to add a word of caution here that it would be utterly impossible to classify Javed Iqbal's TBI exactly without pertinent medical information. There could be a few other syndromes that may be mistaken for coma and obviously the outcome is different but my intention is to make my point that it is very common to find changes in psychosocial behaviour after sustaining a severe TBI.

Various types of cognitive deficits that are common after a TBI are as follows:

Attention and concentration deficit
Judgement and perception problems
Speed and selectivity of information processing
Initiation and goal direction
Learning and memory deficits
Communication problems.

(Mateer CA, Mapou RL, Journal of Head Trauma Rehabilitation 11:78, 1996)

It is also not uncommon to see a wide spectrum of personality changes. These include indifference, dis-inhibition, agitation and sexual inappropriateness as well as changes in judgement and overt aggression. Late neurobehavioral sequelae of a severe TBI may be depression, seizure, schizophrenia, dementia and delayed amnesia. Prognostically, the large majority of those who survive severe TBI have permanent neuropsychological impairments and functional disabilities.

This list of a variety of problems that an individual may run into after an aforementioned happening goes on and on but it is important to recognize and diagnose it clearly to plan for the patient's social living after discharge from hospital. It has an obvious importance in medico-legal circumstances too, that a patient can run into very easily.

Therefore, I can certainly concur with you that Javed Iqbal should have been further investigated medically before any judgement was rendered on his case. In this context it is important that he should have had a CT scan of his head, and neuropsychological and psychiatric evaluations. Any conviction without these evaluations at the minimum does not constitute fairness in my opinion.

D r .   K .   S o h a i l

To sum it up, I think, there are sufficient reasons to suspect that Javed Iqbal sustained a severe traumatic brain injury
due to the beating that he endured, which left him in a possible
coma. Even if he were not in a coma from a technical stand-
point, it would still be possible to sustain a severe traumatic
brain injury. Within a wide variety of sequelae of this type of
injury, it is possible to develop pathological changes in personality, social behaviour and physical and biochemical deficits in
the brain that would be manifested in various ways.

Focusing on the personality problem, I would like to mention that the bizarre kind of thinking process, irrational
judgements and behavioral abnormalities are part of psychosocial pathology that we witness in Javed Iqbal.

Sincerely

Tahir Qazi, MD
Clinical Associate Professor
Department of Physical Medicine and Rehabilitation
University of Saskatoon,
Saskatoon, Saskatchewan, Canada

---

*Criteria to designate TBI as severe are as follows:
1. Glasgow Coma Scale 3-8 at the lowest point after resuscitation (Braddom: Physical Medicine and Rehabilitation p 1031)
2. Length of coma more than 6-8 hours (Eisenberg HM; Outcome after head injury: General Considerations and Neurobehavioural Recovery Part 1 1985)
3. Post-traumatic amnesia more than 24 hours (Ellemberg JH, Saydjari c. PTA as a predictor of outcome after Severe CHI Arch Neurolol 53: 782-791 1996)
4. Skull fracture and hematoma.

PSYCHIATRIC OPINION

After finishing my investigations, I sent a 40-page psychiatric assessment to Mr. Najeeb Faisal Chaudhry, Javed Iqbal's lawyer, in which I summarized my findings, shared my clinical impressions and made various recommendations. Some of the highlights of my assessment and formulation are as follows:

BEGINNING OF CONFLICT

Javed Iqbal, who had been brought up in a loving and nurturing family and was well liked by others in school, faced his first major crisis in life when he was abused by one of his teachers in high school. Javed Iqbal shared in his interview that his teacher Master Riaz always treated him badly and frequently punished him. Javed Iqbal believed that Master Riaz did not like his older brother, who was also his student at one time, so the teacher was taking out his anger on him. Later Javed Iqbal realized the teacher was also angry with other children. One of the students got so upset with him that one day he put some kerosene on the door, while he was with his students, including Javed Iqbal, and put a match to it. Luckily no one was hurt but Javed Iqbal was furious to learn that the teacher blamed him for setting up the other student to do it. He felt wrongly accused by that teacher. That feeling of being wrongly accused stayed with Javed Iqbal for the rest of his life.

INDEPENDENCE AT AN EARLY AGE

Javed Iqbal's older brother Pervaiz Iqbal told me that their father encouraged his children to be emotionally and financially independent as soon as possible. So he arranged marriages for his two sons and a daughter, all at the same time, when they were teenagers. He wanted them to live on their own with their spouses and have a house and business of their own. Pervaiz started a business in Shadbagh. His father asked him to introduce Javed Iqbal to the business when he was barely fourteen. Pervaiz Iqbal felt that when the two older brothers left home, Javed Iqbal lost his supervision. After he had been trained on the job for a couple of years, he and Pervaiz Iqbal got into a conflict. Their father suggested to Pervaiz Iqbal that he hand over the Shadbagh business to

Dr. K. Sohail

Javed Iqbal and move to the Brandrath Road business. Pervaiz Iqbal complied. So Javed Iqbal became an independent businessman as a teenager, while still attending college. During his college days, he got involved in anti-government demonstrations and during one of the confrontations with police, he got injured so badly that he had to be taken to the hospital. When he came out of the hospital, he could not continue with his education and became a full time businessman.

Javed Iqbal wanted to be the leader rather than the follower. He wanted to be the centre of attention. So he started helping the poor, the less privileged, the vulnerable. He also wanted to reform society and wished people to receive fair and just treatment. So he joined Shadbagh Business Association and within a short time became a respectable name in his community. People were quite impressed by his volunteer work. But that phase did not last very long and he faced a major turmoil in his life.

THE DISATROUS MARRIAGE

His marriage was the first major crisis of Javed Iqbal's adult life. On one hand, he felt a pressure from his traditionally-minded family to get married because it was " the right thing to do;" on the other hand, when he chose a woman he wanted to get married to, the family opposed it because she was from a different tribe. The conflict between Javed Iqbal and his family became so tense that he threatened suicide. One of his uncles got so concerned by that threat that he talked to other relatives, asking them to give Javaid Iqbal their blessings to marry that woman. So there was a grand wedding with all the dignitaries in attendance.

As a psychiatrist, I wonder whether the suicidal threat was an immature assertion of independence from family, a genuine cry for help or an act of manipulation? Was Javaid Iqbal emotionally blackmailing the family? Javed Iqbal's dear ones were gradually realizing that he always got his own way. Some felt that his father spoiled him. Generally, his family members and friends gave him what he wanted. Yet the marriage, which had been celebrated with great pomp and show, did not last more than a few months and his wife, though pregnant by him, left him.

Why did she leave? What made her unhappy? What was the major conflict between them? Various people would answer those questions differently based on their perceptions. Pervaiz Iqbal, the older brother, believes that Javed Iqbal's wife, being the eldest family member in Pakistan (the other relatives lived in Saudi Arabia), had the responsibility for looking after her younger siblings. She asked Javed Iqbal to live with her family, but he being a proud man, felt humiliated by the idea of living with his in-laws as ghar jawai.

Javed Iqbal's wife told the police that she had left him because she had seen him having sex with a young boy.

Javed Iqbal's neighbour told me that she had left him because he tried to sodomize her repeatedly.

Javed Iqbal's sexual life was a major factor in creating a conflict between Javed Iqbal and his family and community, a conflict that generated a lot of pain, anger, resentment and even bitterness.

HOMOSEXUAL ENCOUNTERS

Javed Iqbal was involved in homosexual encounters starting in his teenage years. The objects of his lust were young boys and that created a lot of problems for him. Before long he acquired a reputation of child molester; even his brothers would not trust him with their children. When he was caught, he was publicly humiliated in his neighbourhood. Mohammad Aslam Darvesh, president of the Business association, told me, "Once when he was sexually abusing someone we caught him and beat him publicly with slippers to humiliate him. We asked him to write an apology and promise that he would not do it again and that he would leave the market."

It seems very clear that the man who was a bright student and well liked as a volunteer worker had become an outcast within a short time. The famous one became infamous, the saint, a sinner, when he started acting out his sexual impulses and fantasies. His sexuality cost him not only his marriage but also his reputation.

It is interesting how Javed Iqbal was successful in silencing the parents of abused young boys by filling their pockets with money. Javed Iqbal by that time had discovered that he did not have to face the legal consequences of his actions because he was rich.

Homosexuality is a taboo in Pakistani society and is considered illegal, immoral and unnatural. There is never an open dialogue about human sexuality in that culture. There is no sex education in schools and no discussion between children and their parents. There is an atmosphere of judgement rather than a process of acceptance, punishment rather than support and understanding. There is no distinction between homosexual encounters between two consenting adults and an adult and a child. Both acts are considered immoral and illegal.

According to the World Human Rights Guide, Pakistan is one of the countries in the world that has the most serious punishments for homosexual encounters. For example, a Sarghoda judge sentenced a man to seven years imprisonment and 60,000 rupees fine for a homosexual encounter. Failure to pay the fine would result in a further sentence of five years rigorous imprisonment.

Since there is no open discussion about human sexuality in the school or homes, most people are quite ill informed about the subject. They do not have a scientific attitude or psychological understanding about the homosexual lifestyle. Many feel it is because of lack of heterosexual opportunities in a sexually segregated society.

Javed Iqbal's family blamed his failed marriage for his homosexuality. As Pervaiz Iqbal noted in his interview, "Being a married man he must have had some physical needs and when they were not met in the marriage, maybe he went astray. In his workshop he had some young boys." Javed Iqbal started having sexual relationships with them and got himself in big trouble. Javed Iqbal's family never understood and accepted that his sexual activities with boys reflected his preference, rather than desperation.

As well as being punished and persecuted, Javed Iqbal was asked to leave the area. So he started a new business. First he opened a school for children. It was the first air-conditioned school in that area. Later on he started up a video-store mostly for children and teenagers. He was successful in his work financially, but he became quite notorious for manipulating and abusing children. People started avoiding him. They lost their trust in him and no longer respected him.

Javed Iqbal's homosexual activities continued to the extent that in 1990 he was charged with sodomy. It was a nightmare for the whole family because Javed Iqbal had himself disappeared, leaving the family to deal with the fall-out. Unfortunately the family did not see it coming and their experience with the police devastated them, especially his elderly father who was a well-respected man in the community. He was extremely embarrassed on behalf of his son who had been sentenced to time in jail.

SECOND MARRIAGE

After Javed Iqbal was released from jail, his family made one last attempt to reconcile his marriage, but his wife refused to go back to him. Her family gave Javed Iqbal permission to have a second wife.

With Javed Iqbal free in the community again, "... my dad was worried that he might get involved in homosexual encounters again, so we tried to mend their marriage," Pervaiz Iqbal stated in his interview. "The whole family put their heads together. We approached his wife many times but she refused to go back to him. She said she hated him. She even had a daughter from that marriage. Her father gave his word that they would have no objection if Javed Iqbal had a second wife."

It is noteworthy that his first wife did not ask for divorce because she did not want to suffer dire consequences as a divorced woman in the community.

Not accepting his homosexuality, Javed Iqbal's family wanted him to get married the second time. He complied once again but it turned out to be another disaster. His second wife, like the first, left him within a few months, pregnant. The only difference was that when she realized that she could not live with him, she asked for a divorce and cut all ties with him. Like the first wife, she raised their son as a single mother.

There is no evidence to suggest that Javed Iqbal was attached to any of his children. He never made any special effort to be part of their lives. They did not see him for years.

It is quite apparent that Javed Iqbal's family did not understand his sexual problems. They were in denial. That is why the more they tried to help, the worse the situation became. They tried to make him lead a heterosexual life, but they failed miserably. Javed Iqbal told me that the saint had told his father not to force him to get married and lead a straight life.

Dr. K. Sohail

DEATH OF FATHER

Javed Iqbal's father could not take it any longer. The failure of his son's second marriage left him completely devastated. He realized he could not help him. He already had cardiac problems. "Because of all that, Dad was so upset that he had another heart attack and finally died on July 17th, 1992," Pervaiz Iqbal told me.

Losing his father must have been a major crisis for Javed Iqbal, because his father had helped him through thick and thin. He even wrote to him when he was in jail and tried to reassure him of his love and support.

After the father's death, the family gradually withdrew. They gave Javed Iqbal his share of the inheritance and then distanced themselves.

CLOSE TIES WITH POLICE

Once when his family went to his new residence to attend a memorial service for his father, they were surprised to see police cruisers outside and uniformed officers in the house. They were worried he might have got into trouble again, but were shocked to find out that he was their friend. Javed Iqbal's family did not like his socializing with the police. They believed that since the police were corrupt, the only people who kept close ties with them were those who were involved in illegal activities.

Javed Iqbal was not ashamed or embarrassed, but instead, quite pleased and proud of his association with the police. He became so involved in their activities that he started publishing an anti-corruption newspaper and in it featured pictures of his favourite police officers.

Darvesh said in his interview, "Once I was sitting in the office of Shahab-ud-din, SHO [Station House Officer] of the Shadbagh Police, when Javed Iqbal came with a friend and threw a magazine on the desk and said, 'See, I am publishing this impressive magazine. I have included your pictures.' He used to manipulate everybody especially with his money."

Javed Iqbal started living closer and closer to the edge. On one hand he had connections with law-breakers and on the other with law enforcers. He was friends with both parties, both sides; he kept the balance for a while but then started to lose the ability to maintain it.

CHARGES OF SODOMY

In 1998 he was again charged with sodomy. Javed Iqbal's brother believes that he was framed. He stated, "Javed Iqbal said those people owed him money, and when he demanded his money back, they made false accusations and framed him in a sodomy case. Since he had been charged before with the same offence, it was easier to make another case."

Whatever the facts might have been, it seems obvious that Javed Iqbal had made enemies who were determined to hurt him one way or another. Javed Iqbal's relationship with his friends and family members had become an angry, resentful and bitter one. The tension kept mounting as Javed Iqbal was approaching a breaking point in his life. He was getting close to the breakdown of his relationships.

FINAL BREAKDOWN

In 1998, Javed Iqbal had such a breakdown that he was in a coma for twenty-two days. One morning his neighbours in Fatehgarh heard some cries, and when they entered the house, they found Javed Iqbal and twelve-year-old Arbab unconscious. They were taken to two different hospitals. Nobody believed Javed Iqbal would live. But the miracle happened and he survived. He was so badly beaten up by his employees that he had multiple fractures of his skull and jaw.

After he had marginally recovered from life-threatening injuries, he was prematurely discharged from the hospital. There were no plans for his rehabilitation. His family took him to another hospital but they were "treated like animals." Finally they took him to a dental hospital where his jaw was operated upon but not his skull. Javed Iqbal was quite disillusioned by the hospital and the health-care system. He was further upset by the fact that the man who tried to kill him was not charged. He became angry with the police.

That whole incident made him so upset that his anger, resentment and bitterness turned into revenge.

He was also disappointed in his family for refusing to pay the fee for a private hospital. His brother stated that even assessment and initial treatment would have cost them 96,000 rupees, which they could not afford. The family by then had decided not to get involved in his affairs and to let him face the consequences of his actions. Javed Iqbal was burning his bridges one by one.

Javed Iqbal was becoming aware that his mother was the only person left in his entire life that loved and accepted him unconditionally. She looked after him when he was sick and recovering from his injuries. He wrote in his diary,

"On the 8th of October, 1998, when I regained my consciousness, I was lying in my mother's house. Mom told me that I was sick and that I had experienced a major crisis. With the grace of God I regained consciousness after 22 days...During that time, the only person who stayed with me and supported me was my mother."

The following year, his mother herself fell ill. His diary notes:

"July 9th, 1999. Doctors are trying their best to keep my mom alive with the help of machines. I take a rickshaw and visit my mom every day. I stay in the hospital from morning to evening. My brothers, sisters and sisters-in-law come and spend some time with Mom in the hospital. From the 5th of July, I have been spending time there. I told Iqbal, whom I have helped since his childhood, that I am spending the last days of my life."

"July 26th, 1999. Mom died today. It is hell for me. Mom was everything to me. My worries killed my mom. My murderers, by trying to kill me, also killed my mother. I will take revenge by making hundreds of other mothers suffer. With the help of God I will succeed in my plan. I tried to help homeless boys but they tried to kill me. One of them was caught, but the police officer protected him by giving him refuge in his own house. After the news of my killings gets public, I will see how that officer protects himself. I do not have any hope in people or the police to do justice...I am ready to take my revenge."

The Myth of the Chosen One

It is obvious that Javed Iqbal's loss of hope in the justice system and his sense of betrayal by his employees, friends and relatives were significant factors in transforming his anger into revenge.

Javed Iqbal's mother's death broke his heart. That was the last straw. After that he did not care for anything or anybody.

A BROKEN MAN

Following the death of his mother, he became a broken man in more than one way. He was not only physically crippled; he was also emotionally bankrupt. That must have been the lowest point of his life. He lost his health, wealth, self-esteem and faith in life.

He felt so devastated and depressed, he wanted to die, to kill himself, to commit suicide, but then he became so angry that he made a master plan to take revenge, the ultimate revenge. While his mother was sick, he had already made a plan, but his mother's death accelerated the process.

Javed Iqbal kept a diary and wrote the details of his plans to kidnap homeless boys, bring them to his newly rented home on Ravi Road, Lahore, and kill them. He decided that if he had drums full of acid then he could put the dead bodies in them and they would dissolve. According to his diary, he convinced some young boys to help him with his master plan. He describes how he paid them money and let them abuse and kill the boys. His gang allegedly brought those young boys from Data Darbar or Minar-e-Pakistan, gave them sedatives, put them to sleep and then strangled them.

Javed Iqbal had planned to kill one hundred boys. When that mission was completed, he handed over his diaries, with all the details of the killings and the 57 pictures he had taken of those boys to the Inspector General of Police and local journalists. In the beginning he had a hard time convincing them that he had done all the killings. He told the police that he had guns, chains, drugs, drums full of acid and parts of dead bodies in those drums, but nobody believed him. They all thought he was a liar, a little eccentric, even crazy. He had a hard time making them take him seriously.

Dr. K. Sohail

In this whole ordeal, the role of police was quite bizarre and irresponsible. Javed Iqbal's account of that in his diary, smacks of black humour.

"*Finally a stage came in my life when it was a disgrace for me to live. Then I prayed to God to give me enough power and courage to destroy the whole world. I decided to kill 100, not 101. When I finished my project of killing 100, I wrote a letter to DIG Police on November 22nd, 1999. Nobody took me seriously. They thought I was lying.*

"*One day DSP Tariq Camboh came to my house with a whole bunch of commandos. They surrounded my house but before they broke in, I opened the door voluntarily. I had decided to shoot myself with my Point 22 pistol. Tariq Camboh said he came to see me. There were police inspectors with him. First they ordered, "hands up", but after they saw my face they got scared. I put the pistol to my temple as my mission had been completed. Tariq Camboh said he read my letter to the police. At that time dead bodies were present in my house.*

"*After a while Tariq Camboh said, 'Go to sleep. Take it easy. Go to sleep." His behavior surprised me. Then I gave my pistol to Tariq Camboh. But he refused to take it. One of the inspectors came forward and took my pistol.*

"*Then Tariq Camboh said, ' I am sorry we came to bother you.' I was shocked to hear that. Then he said, 'We came here to help you.' Then he picked up one of my bags and asked, 'What is this?' Then he picked one of my chains and said, 'They look dangerous!' and put them back.*

"*Before Tariq Camboh left, he said again, 'Go to sleep. Have some rest. Come to the police station tomorrow morning.'*

"*Which police station?" I asked.*

"*CIA Qilla Gujar Singh,' he answered.*

"*The next day I went to the police station where they had arrested Sajid. They let Sajid go with me.*"

The police started looking for Javed Iqbal on December 2nd, 1999, after he had mysteriously disappeared, but then it was too late. He was one step ahead of the police. People who knew him were confident the police would not be able to catch him and he would surrender on his own. Meanwhile, the police illegally arrested his family members for investigation and kept them in custody.

Mr. Butt, the neighbour, said in his interview, "We were also sure that the police would never be able to catch him. One day when he would decide, then he would surrender voluntarily. And that was actually happened in the end. The police had kept his brothers and nephews in custody while they were searching for Javed Iqbal."

Javed Iqbal finally appeared in the office of Jang Newspaper on the evening of December 30, 1999 and made confessions to the journalists. He offered himself to the police. On December 31, his pictures were front-page news in every newspaper, and he was declared the worst killer of the century. He was arrested, kept in police custody, charged and finally convicted on March 16, 2000 of killing one hundred children. The interesting part was that in spite of confessions, when Javed Iqbal appeared in front of the judge, he and his disciples pleaded not guilty.

TO BELIEVE OR NOT TO BELIEVE

When I read the verdict, it appeared to me that the judge had based his punishment based on the following:

1. Javed Iqbal's diaries which he submitted to the police.
2. Javed Iqbal's posters that police found in his house (handwriting experts confirmed that they were written by Javed Iqbal).
3. Pictures of boys that Javed Iqbal submitted with the diaries.
4. Clothes and shoes that were kept by Javed Iqbal in his house and which were identified by the family members of belonging to those boys.
5. Confessions that Javed Iqbal made to journalists.

I strongly believe that in Javed Iqbal's diaries, letters and confessions, facts and fiction, reality and fantasy are so intricately woven together that it is hard to know what are truths, what are confabulations and what are lies. My interview with his nephew Waseem highlighted that the murder of a young girl on November 6th, 1999 was a fragment of Javed Iqbal's imagination rather than a reality.

I was quite surprised that the judge never ordered a formal examination by a team of psychologists and psychiatrists before giving his verdict. I have serious doubts about the authenticity of the diaries.

After reviewing Javed Iqbal's diaries and confessions and the role of the police, who were subsequently charged with the murder of Ishaq Billa, a key witness to Javed Iqbal's case, I strongly feel that the judge came to the verdict in great haste. The case started in February 2000 and ended in March 2000.

The judge was quick to acknowledge, "It is an admitted fact that the present case is totally based on circumstantial evidence and there exists no direct evidence in this case." Even the body parts discovered in the drums from Javed Iqbal's house were not proven to be of human origin. The judge also stated that the case was decided, "within the shortest possible time as directed by Mian Muhammad Jahangir, learned District and Sessions Judge, Lahore, for the expeditious disposal of this case."

I feel that if the judge had given the case more time, consideration and thought, he might have come to a different verdict.

DIAGNOSTIC IMPRESSIONS

PERSONALITY DISORDER

After interviewing Javed Iqbal, his family members and neighbours, and reviewing all the evidence and documents available to me, I am of the opinion that Javed Iqbal suffers from a serious Personality Disorder.

According to *The Diagnostic and Statistical Manual of Mental Disorders (DSM IV)* published by American Psychiatric Association, the general diagnostic criteria for a Personality Disorder are:

a) An enduring pattern of inner experience and behaviour that deviates markedly from the expectations of the individual's culture. This pattern is manifested in two or more of the following areas:

1. cognition (i.e., ways of perceiving and interpreting self, other people and events)

2. affectivity (i.e., the range, intensity, lability and appropriateness of emotional responses)

3. interpersonal functioning

4. impulse control

b) The enduring pattern is inflexible and pervasive across a broad range of personal and social situations.

c) The enduring pattern leads to clinically significant distress or impairment in social, occupational or other important areas of functioning.

d) The pattern is stable and of long duration and its onset can be traced back at least to adolescence or early adulthood.

e) The enduring pattern is not better accounted for as a manifestation or consequence of another mental disorder

f) The enduring pattern is not due to the direct physiological effects of a substance (drug abuse, medication) or a general medical condition.

In my opinion, Javed Iqbal's Personality Disorder has the characteristics of:

NARCISSISM

Javed Iqbal is very ego-centric and has a grandiose self image. He, from his childhood, felt he was special. He believed he had special spiritual and creative powers and deserved special treatment from others. He considered himself "The Chosen One." Whenever his narcissism was injured he started to threaten and manipulate others around him. Aslam Darvesh, who knew Javed Iqbal most of his life, stated, "He is more of a narcissistic person than a criminal. He likes to promote himself by exaggerating things."

PSYCHOPATHIC AND ANTISOCIAL BEHAVIOUR

Javed Iqbal showed no remorse or guilt. He did not appear to have a conscience. "Our hearts have turned into stone," he wrote in his diaries. He justified all his behaviour and found convoluted rationalizations for his behaviour. He obviously lacks awareness of the effects of his behaviour on others.

He was never reluctant to break social traditions and legal norms. Whenever he broke the law, he tried to hide behind his wealth and social contacts. He never accepted responsibility for his behaviour. Whenever he was caught, rather than confessing his illegal action, he insisted that it was a "misunderstanding".

PEDOPHILIA

From his teenage years he was sexually interested in young boys. Although he was married twice because of the pressures of the family, both of those marriages failed miserably within a few months. He was always surrounded with young boys. His charismatic personality seemed to have a special impact on young minds. He had a cultish personality and his disciples seemed to be so loyal to him that they were willing to face jail or even death rather than be unfaithful to him. Alongside having sexual contacts with teenagers, there is also a history with children. Some psychologists feel that many pedophiles have all the characteristics of psychopaths. They just manipulate children and use sex as a method of exploitation.

DEPRESSION

Javed Iqbal experienced episodes of depression after his hospitalization and felt suicidal many times. He even made plans to shoot himself or drown himself in Ravi River but then decided not to act on his impulses. His depression, I believe, was precipitated by the significant losses in his life and some of that depression was transformed into anger, resentment, bitterness and, ultimately, revenge.

DRUG ABUSE

There is some evidence that Javed Iqbal sometimes abused street and prescription drugs. Police found some tablets and unknown drugs from his house. Even when he was arrested there were some "intoxicant" tablets in his socks. During his interview he shared an episode when he experienced visual hallucinations.

BRAIN DAMAGE

As Javed Iqbal was in a coma for twenty-two days, I strongly suspect that there was some brain damage. I believe that in his diaries, some day-to-day realities were intermingled with lies and confabulations because of cognitive damage after severe traumatic head injuries. He wrote in his diary, "I was in a coma for 22 days. I am in such a miserable state that I can hardly walk or eat or see. I have a broken jaw. The fractures of my skull keep me disoriented."

RECOMMENDATION

I had suggested to the lawyer that Javed Iqbal's case needed to be re-investigated and that he be examined by a multi-disciplinary team of doctors, psychologists and psychiatrists before it was too late.

⌧ 16 *The Mystery of the Cultish Personality*

"It is dangerous because it is out to capture people, especially children and impressionable young people and indoctrinate and brainwash them so that they become the unquestioning captives and tools of the cult, withdrawn, from ordinary thought, living and relationship with others."

Mr. Justice Latey, rendering an assessment
of Scientology in the High Court.

While I was writing my psychiatric assessment I became aware that personalities like Javed Iqbal are so complex that they transcend traditional classifications. I remembered what Shamsheer Khan had commented, when I asked his impression of Javed Iqbal. He had said, "He is not an ordinary prisoner. He is very deep." The depth that he was referring to and the extent to which his personality and lifestyle have affected his family and community are very intriguing and profound. I feel the labels of Psychopathic, Sociopathic and Antisocial Personality Disorder do not do justice to his character. It is not that he does not have those characteristics, it is that he has more than that. The question I ask myself is,"What does Javed Iqbal have that other psychopaths do not have?" I believe he has some characteristics of those rare people who if they succeed, become leaders of cults. That is why I believe that Javed Iqbal, like a few others in every century, has a Cultish Personality.

People with Cultish Personalities are not only very charismatic, they also lead non-traditional lives because of their unconventional philosophies and belief systems. They continually challenge the taboos and confront traditions, which causes them to run afoul of legal, religious and social institutions. It is not uncommon to see them challenging the spiritual, social and sexual norms. They are generally creative and many of their activities are seen as unethical, abnormal and even criminal. Because of their charm and charisma they have a following. It is not difficult for them to attract very dedicated disciples. These disciples who are generally young and vulnerable human beings are willing to give enormous sacrifices for their leader and call him their guru or prophet. Over a period of time the following grows. Unfortunately when the guru is penalized and persecuted, the followers also suffer.

Thus, when Javed Iqbal got into legal trouble his teenage disciples and lovers had to face persecution too. One of them, Ishaq Billa, gave his life; the others are facing execution and life sentences. Javed Iqbal's older brother Pervaiz stated in his interview, "In the present case the police tried their best but the boys took his side. They might be hanged in the process but they are still faithful to him. They are so faithful that the whole world is astonished." The younger brother Saeed said, "He succeeds in convincing others of whatever he wants even if he is lying."

When I think of other personalities in the last century who I believe had Cultish Personalities, the first person that comes to my mind is Gregory Rasputin, the mad monk of Siberia. In the early part of the twentieth century, Rasputin became a mythological figure in Russian politics. He had a number of characteristics that made him extraordinary. He was loved and hated by millions of Russians. He started his career as a religious minister in Siberia but gradually he became famous in the country because of his hypnotic and healing powers. When Tsar Nicholas and Tsaritza Alexandra found out that their son suffered from Hemophilia and could not be cured by doctors, one of the maids suggested to the Tzaritza that she should consult Rasputin. When Rasputin was summoned, the young prince was so sick, that the doctors were worried he would die because of continuous bleeding. Rasputin asked all the physicians present to leave and spent half an hour with the child on his own. When the Tsar and Tsaritza came into the room, they were amazed to see their son smiling and playing. The Tsaritza was so impressed by the healing miracle that she became Rasputin's disciple. Although Tsar Nicholas was suspicious of Rasputin's intentions, the Tsaritza continued to invite him to the palace.

Over the years Rasputin became a major political influence in the Tsar's family and political life. Rasputin himself led a very dissolute life; he slept with married and single women indiscriminately, drank excessively and at times got violent and abusive. This behaviour made him many enemies who attempted to kill him by various means; ultimately he was poisoned, shot and drowned in a dramatic finale. Historians hold Rasputin partly responsible for the downfall of the Tsar. It has been said that if there had been no Rasputin, there would have been no Lenin. Gradually Rasputin became a mythological figure because of his Cultish Personality. He has become part of world folklore. Boney M, a popular music group of 1970s, in their song Rasputin sing,

"Ra Ra Rasputin, Russia's greatest love machine.

Ra Ra Rasputin, lover of the Russian Queen..."

From my readings, I do not believe that Rasputin was ever sexually involved with the Empress, but it is one aspect of the Cultish Personality that in folklore, the facts and fiction, fantasy and reality, all become intricately intertwined.

In the second half of the twentieth century there were a number of men in America who became famous and notorious because of their Cultish Personalities. Some, like David Koresh, attracted only a few hundred disciples, while others like Sung Myung Moon, the prophet of the so-called "Moonies" and L. Ron Hubbard, guru of the Church of Scientology, have attracted millions as their disciples. Moon is well known for conducting wedding ceremonies in which thousands of men and women get married simultaneously because it has been arranged by their prophet. Sometimes the spouses do not even speak the same language. It is because, "to join the Moonies is to abrogate almost all responsibility for personal decision-making," even the choice of the partner. (Ref. 1 p 75)

David Berg who started his cult with the "life of ease, drugs and spirituality" by "combining religion and pop music" (Ref. 1 p 114) and calling his disciples Children of God, gradually became a focus of resentment and ridicule when he took a mistress and started preaching free sex. As the cult deteriorated, the spirituality was transformed into sexuality. "Women members were, in effect, required to prostitute themselves in clubs, bars and other social meeting places for sake of recruitment, irrespective of whether they were married or single. 'Sex for Jesus' became the buzz-phrase until the late 1980's, when the spread of AIDS made it unrealistic." The cult got into real trouble when members started having sexual relationships with the children as their prophet believed, "There is no laws against incest in the loving Kingdom of God."

David Koresh was a follower of a Bulgarian-born immigrant to America, Victor Houteff, who started his Branch Davidian sect as an offshoot of the mainstream Seventh Day Adventists in 1929. David Koresh took over the cult in 1986.

> "He introduced ideas of polygamy, group upbringing of commune children, violent resistance to outside authorities and, most significantly, the idea that he was the bearer of the final message of God and the key to the Seventh Seal of the Book of Revelation by which the faithful would be marked and saved from doom."

Koresh got into legal trouble because his disciples began collecting arms in their commune and when they refused to surrender to the police, the cult compound was attacked by the FBI and all but two members perished in the ensuing fire on April 19th, 1993.

One Cultish Personality who became well-known in North America was Guru Rajneesh. He was a professor of philosophy in India. Because of his intelligence and mesmerizing personality he had a number of disciples. Gradually he started preaching meditation and free sex and thousands of Westerners who were exploring alternate lifestyles joined his Ashram. But when his philosophy and teachings were criticized by local people, he had to leave India.

> *"He had also managed to attract considerable antagonism on the sub-continent for his hostility and derogation of others, including Gandhi and Mother Teresa of Calcutta. His self-styled title of 'Bhagwan' [which means God and also Master of Vagina] and his overseeing of naked, sexually-charged romps on the seashore brought more local disfavor."*
>
> Cults, Michael Jordan, England 1996.

Rajneesh was forced to relocate to the United States where he established his own commune. For a while he was so successful that he had accumulated, among other trappings of wealth, a fleet of 99 Rolls Royces. However, he got into legal difficulties with the local community and was asked to leave the country. Unfortunately his motherland refused to take him so for a few years he wandered around in different parts of the world until his death in 1990, "allegedly as a result of either poisoning or from full blown AIDS." (Ref. 1 p 65). In the years since his death, millions of people have visited his Ashram in India. Interestingly the leader of the movement is a Canadian by the name of Swami Mike, son of a British Columbia judge. According to one report, the average revenue generated in that Ashram in Poona, India, is nearly 50 million dollars a year.

Like many other Cultish Personalities of this century, Javed Iqbal has also been successful in creating a myth, a myth in which it is very difficult to differentiate between fact and fiction, fantasy and reality.

Is he a sinner?

Is he a criminal or a messiah?

Did he want to destroy or reform his community?

The more I investigated the story, the more I came to the realization that there were no realities, only perceptions. In his own eyes he is a saint, *The Chosen One*, in the eyes of neighbours a sinner, in the eyes of the community a criminal and in the eyes of the judge a Satan.

Gradually I realized that in Javed Iqbal's life, his creativity, spirituality, sexuality and criminality all became intimately intertwined. Truth got mixed with deception and eventually the story became so bizarre, so surrealistic that the two could not be separated. For Javed Iqbal to choose to go to the newspaper office on December 30th, 1999 and appear on the front page of national newspapers on December 31st, 1999 might reflect a hidden desire to be known as "Serial Killer of the Millennium."

☒ 17 *Thousands of Children Missing*

"What's done to children, they will do to society."

— Karl A Menninger

As I pondered over Javed Iqbal's story, I realized that it was not the story of just one man, it was the story of the whole nation. It was the story of all those families who lost their children and all those teachers whose students were missing from the classrooms and all those police stations that did not investigate the stories of missing children. It was amazing that not one single case of those missing children was reported in any police station in the country. Some parents complained that they approached the local police stations but the case was not registered because they could not afford bribes for the officers. It seemed as though there was a pervasive apathy in every level of society.

When the Human Rights Commission of Pakistan interviewed the families of missing children, they published the following report in the Dawn Internet Newspaper.

"Islamabad, June 14, 2000. The Human Rights Commission of Pakistan (HRCP), holding society's indifference also responsible for the tragedy of 100 children who were killed in Lahore by a self-confessed criminal, has called for legislation to check the exploitation of missing/runaway children.

"The Commission's conclusion is based on a survey it conducted of the victims' families who flocked to Lahore after Javed Iqbal Mughal revealed to a newspaper how he killed the children and dissolved their bodies in acid. The objective of the survey, which covered 48 victims, was to ascertain the socio-economic factors that could have contributed to this ghastly episode.

"It showed that one person alone could not be blamed for the liquidation of scores of young lives. It was also a fact that the parents and families of the victims too did not make or were unable to make adequate efforts to trace the runaway children, the educational institutions failed to win the confidence of the pupils who disappeared during enrolment at schools/madaris or after giving up their studies, and the police took little interest in tracing the missing children".

While Javed Iqbal was making headlines in the press, the Commission reported that the fate of 6000 missing children in Punjab alone was not known. This list may have grown longer over the last few months covering the entire country.

Expecting that these revelations would shake the administration and the public out of their negligence in dealing with such children, the HRCP stressed the urgent need to create a system under which missing or runaway children can be traced with the determination that the matter merits.

One of the puzzling questions is what happened to those 100 children that were missing, according to Javed Iqbal's story. If they had not been murdered by Javed Iqbal, as many lay people and professionals that I talked to believed, then where did they go? Some believe they were sold to rich Arabs to ride in the famous yearly Camel Races, where the jockeys are small boys. Others suspected that they had been sold to rich

Westerners who needed organ transplants. While I was wondering whether there could be any truth to those rumours, I came across the following in a Canadian newspaper, The Sunday Sun, October 29, 2000.

BOY'S ORGANS FOR SALE
Russians Arrest Grandmother
MOSCOW(AP) The boy thought his grandmother was taking him to Disneyland, but Russian police say she had other plans—to sell her grandson so his organs could be used for transplants.

Police in Ryazan, 200 km south-east of Moscow, said yesterday they arrested a woman after they were tipped that she was trying to sell her grandson to a man who was going to take the boy to the West. There, his organs were to be removed and sold, a Ryazan police officer said.

After a surveillance operation, police moved in to arrest the woman Tuesday, capturing the event on a videotape that was released in part yesterday, Police did not reveal the woman's name.

The woman was helped in the scheme by the boy's uncle, who told police the child was being sold for about US$70,000.

When asked how he could sell his nephew, the uncle replied: "My mother said that it is none of my business, he is her grandson." The boy, whose age was not released, lived with his grandmother.

Body parts have been smuggled out of Russia in the past for sale in the West as organ replacements."

If such an incident happened in Moscow, could it also happen in Pakistan?

It is unfortunate that even in the twenty-first century there are a number of conservative countries where a homosexual lifestyle is illegal and a number of communities all over the world where sexual relationships between two men or two women are considered, immoral, sinful and unnatural. In such communities gay and lesbian men and women are punished, penalized, humiliated and ostracized. Many of them feel vulnerable to being deported, sent to jail for years or even sentenced to death.

Such judgmental and punitive reactions are the result of moralistic traditions and religious attitudes of people and communities who not only disapprove of all homosexual relationships but also deny their blessing to heterosexual encounters that do not take place inside the institution of marriage. Most of them believe that the only role sex plays in human life is reproduction. They object to all forms of recreational sex whether between homosexual or heterosexual couples.

In the last couple of centuries in the progressive countries and liberal societies of the West, there has been a gradual acceptance of gay and lesbian lifestyles. Some of the factors that paved the way for such acceptance are as follows:

1. The lifestyles of a number of prominent individuals propelled the issue into the news media for mainstream people to discuss. When Oscar Wilde was sentenced to jail in England for his homosexual encounters, there were a number of writers, artists and human rights activists who objected to that sentence, and when the movie star Rock Hudson acknowledged publicly that he suffered from AIDS, more and more Americans started talking publicly about homosexuality and AIDS.

2. There were a number of fictional and non-fictional books written in the twentieth century about human sexuality in general and homosexuality in particular that attracted public attention.

Dr. K. Sohail

3. Psychologists like Freud stated that homosexuality was not a part of mental illness. "Homosexuality is assuredly no advantage, but it is nothing to be ashamed of, no vice, no degradation. It cannot be classified as an illness. We consider it to be a variation of the sexual function. Many highly respectable individuals of ancient and modern times have been homosexuals." Research workers like Kinsey, through extensive interviews tried to show that homosexuality was an integral part of human nature, and that ten to thirty percent of men and women of America had either indulged in casual homosexual encounters or accepted homosexuality as their preferred choice. There was also a larger number who were bisexuals.

4. There were serious debates among mental health professionals as to whether homosexuality was abnormal and unhealthy or a chosen lifestyle. There was a time homosexuality was included in the international classification of mental disorders but that is no longer the case. It is now considered one of the choices people make in their lives.

5. There have been a number of movements that focusing on human rights of gay and lesbian people that have brought about changes in the laws in different countries. Because of those movements, gay and lesbian men and women are protected from harassment at work and prejudice in the community in most Western countries.

6. The media have also played an important role in this regard. Through newspapers and radio and television programs, more and more people are being educated about human sexuality and encouraged to accept minorities with their alternative lifestyles.

7. Liberal churches have not only accepted gay ministers but have also given their blessings to gay and lesbian couples by performing wedding ceremonies.

Because of those changes in Western societies, more and more people are coming out of the closet and feeling proud of their sexual preferences and alternative lifestyles.

Although gay and lesbian people have come a long way in the Western world in the last century, there remains strong community resistance to their being legally accepted as couples.

In many African, Middle Eastern and Asian countries there is still a lot of ignorance and prejudice regarding sexuality in general. Unfortunately most teachers do not approve of sex education and most parents do not feel comfortable discussing human sexuality with their children. As a result teenagers and even adults find themselves in the dark. Many young homosexuals live in constant fear. Some of them suppress their feelings and feel chronically unhappy and depressed, some get married and stay in the closet, while there are others who become very angry, resentful and bitter. At times that anger and bitterness turns into revenge and such people become physically and sexually abusive.

It is horrifying to know that there are millions of people suffering from AIDS in those countries who do not get proper education or health care. It seems that millions of people all over the world still live in denial.

I strongly feel that in countries like Pakistan there is a great need for:

- sex education as an integral part of the school syllabus for teenagers
- health education for adults to prevent unwanted pregnancies and sexually transmitted diseases
- comprehensive care for people who suffer from AIDS
- feature articles in daily newspapers and programs on radio and television focusing on human sexuality in general and homosexuality in particular, promoting acceptance and respect for people with alternative lifestyles.

I hope sooner, rather than later, that people with alternative lifestyles will be accepted and respected in Pakistan, and that gay and lesbian couples will enjoy the same rights and privileges as heterosexual couples. I hope that we can create an environment which is supportive and sympathetic, rather than judgmental and punitive, towards homosexual individuals and couples.

It is sad to see that while millions of men and women gather every year in Toronto and New York to join the Gay Pride Parade and cele-brate their loving relationships, gay and lesbian men and women in Pakistan still face public humiliation, social ostracism and court-decreed punishments. People in Pakistan still do not differentiate between loving relationships between two adults and abusive relationships between adults and children. When I asked Mr. Minto, the Supreme Court lawyer, whether according to Pakistani law, there is any difference between homosexual encounters between two consenting adults and an adult and a child, he stated, "Well, there is no difference whatsoever. The perpetrator of a crime of sodomy, whether he commits the offence with a child or commits with an adult, he is equally guilty."

It is not uncommon for anyone involved in a homosexual encounter in Pakistan to be heavily fined and sentenced to years in prison.

⬛ 19 The Enigma of Psychopathic Personality

"His hand will be against every man
and every man's hand against him."
— Genesis

INTRODUCTION

People with psychopathic personalities have remained a mystery for professionals as well as lay people over the centuries. It has been diffi-cult for the families and communities of such people to comprehend why, in spite of knowing the difference between right and wrong, these people repeatedly prefer wrong over right. Psychopaths, because of their criminal behaviour and antisocial lifestyles, cause much emotional pain for their families and social suffering for their communities. Ironically, these people do not experience any guilt or shame. They do not learn from their experiences. People around them do not know what to do with them. It is not uncommon for such people to land up in prison due to conflict with the law, because mental health professionals are reluctant to admit them to a psychiatric hospital as they do not have much to offer them. D. Henderson in his book *Psychopathic States* (1939) wrote,

> *"It is often much against his better judgement that the judge sentences a man whose conduct on the face of it indicates the action of an unsound mind to serve a term of imprisonment. But he is almost forced to do so because, according to our present statutes governing commitment, the doctor may not feel that he is justified in certifying the individual as suitable for care and treatment in a mental hospital."*

HISTORY

Although the terms Psychopathic, Sociopathic and Antisocial Personalities are recent, the descriptions of such people can be found in world literature throughout history. The Bible describes a psychopath in these words: *"His mouth is full of curses and lies and threats; trouble and evil are under his tongue. He lies in wait near the villages; from ambush he murders the innocent, watching in secret for his victims. He lies in wait like a lion in cover, he lies in wait to catch the helpless, he catches the helpless and drags them off in his net. His victims are crushed, they collapse: they fall under his strength."* Psalms 10:7-9

One of Aristotle's students, Theophrastus, depicted a personality with some of the psychopathic traits under the title, "The Unscrupulous Man' in these words: "The Unscrupulous Man will go and borrow more money from a creditor he has never paid ... When marketing he reminds the butcher of some service he has rendered him and, standing near the scales, throws in some meat, if he can, and a soup bone. If he succeeds, so much the better, if not, he will snatch a piece of tripe and go off laughing." (Widiger, Corbitt & Millon, 1991, p. 63).

When we study modern developments in mental health we find Philippe Pinel to be one of the pioneers who in the early 19th century tried to focus on these personalities. He described them as those people who behaved in impulsive and self-destructive ways although their reasoning powers were not damaged by mental aberration. They were not suffering from any mental illness but still behaved irrationally and irresponsibly. He described them as suffering from *manie sans delire* (insanity without delirium). Pinel described these personalities who exhibit anti-social behaviours in these words:

> *"Though their crimes may be sickening, they are not sick in either a medical or a legal sense. Instead the serial killer is typically a sociopathic personality who lacks internal contro l— guilt or conscience — to guide his own behaviour, but has an excessive need to control and dominate others. He definitely knows right from wrong, definitely realizes he had committed a sinful act, but simply does not care about his human prey. The sociopath has never internalized a moral code that prohibits murder. Having fun is all that counts."* (Levin & Fox, 1985, p. 229-230)

Pinel seems to have well captured the essence of these person-alities.

Benjamin Rush, an American physician, had also observed in the 19th century that some of his patients had clear thinking and understood the difference between right and wrong but still indulged in socially inappropriate and irresponsible behaviours. He believed they had "innate ... moral depravity."

Even in the nineteenth century, it was apparent that psychopathic personalities had two distinct dimensions, a psychological one and a social one. On one hand such personalities did not feel shame, remorse or guilt, and on the other hand they indulged in antisocial activities and exploited other people.

In the nineteenth century, British psychiatrist J. Prichard coined a term "moral insanity" for such individuals. In 1835 Prichard wrote about such personalities.

> *"There is a form of mental derangement in which the intellectual functions appear to have sustained little or no injury, while the disorder is maintained principally or alone in the state of the feelings, temper or habits. In cases of this nature the moral or active principles of the mind are strongly perverted or depraved; the power of self-government is lost or greatly impaired ...."*

Such discussion differentiated between insane individuals who suffered from delusions, hallucinations and thought disorder and insane people who behaved immorally and irresponsibly but did not suffer from psychosis.

By the end of the nineteenth century some psychiatrists believed that these people have some inborn defect. They were not sure about the nature of this defect but felt that it was not the result of faulty upbringing. Lombrosa coined the expression "born delinquent" while British Psychiatrist Henry Maudsley described them in these words,

> *"As there are persons who cannot distinguish certain colours, having what is called colour blindness, so there are some who are coNgenitally deprived of moral sense."*

It is quite clear that by the end of the nineteenth century, experts were thinking about the nature and the dynamics of psychopathic personalities in a very serious manner and were entertaining different theories as to their etiology. By the turn of the century, the term "moral insanity" was gradually being replaced by "psychopathic inferiority" suggested by J. Koch (1891) and "constitutionally inferior" offered by Adolf Meyer (1904). Meyer was also trying to differentiate psychopathic personalities not only from the psychotics but also from the neurotics. He observed that psychopathic personalities did not suffer from anxiety disorders.

Kraft Ebbing in the early twentieth century focused on sexual lives of psychopathic personalities and showed that such people interact with other human beings out of lust rather than love. They exploit other human beings and use sex to control them. Havelock Ellis also highlighted the sadomasochistic character of their relationships. He observed that psychopathic personalities enjoyed hurting and inflicting pain on people they were sexually involved with.

Kraeplin used the expression "psychopathic states" in his textbook of psychiatry and described the "morally insane" as suffering congenital defects in their ability to restrain the "reckless gratification of... immediate egotistical desires." He believed that these tendencies were pathological and were lifelong.

In the early part of the twentieth century in the Western world, it was generally believed that psychopathic personalities were the result of some inborn defect and any form of training or punishment would not change their lifestyle.

Kurt Schneider, in 1923, published a book *Psychopathic Personalities* in which he outlined his study of their abnormalities and how they affected their lifestyles. He described them in these words, "Their character is a pitiless one and they lack capacity for shame, decency, remorse and conscience. They are ungracious, cold, surly, and brutal in crime." Schneider was also aware that their irresponsible and insensitive behaviour affected not only strangers but also their dear ones. "These 'hotheads' often present a social problem in their disturbed marriages, in their incapacity to care for their children properly and in their criminal outbreaks."

Some psychiatrists were so concerned about the effects of psychopathic personalities on others that they suggested sterilization for such individuals.

August Aichorn in 1925 made some of the early contributions towards psychoanalytic understanding of such personalities. He believed that such individuals were unable to internalize parental and societal norms as children. They could not learn to control their urges and acted very impulsively. Wilhelm Reich believed these people did not develop "super-ego" or conscience, hence the absence of any sense of guilt.

Franz Alexander in 1935 in his book *The Roots of Crime* discussed how the unresolved conflicts of childhood of psychopathic personalities finally turn into anger and resentment and bitterness towards society and are expressed in criminal behaviour.

> *"The emotional conflicts and deprivations of childhood, the resentments of parents and siblings, find a powerful ally in resentment against the social situation, and this combined emotional tension seeks a realistic expression in criminal acts and cannot be relieved by mere fantasy products that are exhibited in neurotic symptoms."*

Harvey Cleckley's book *The Mask of Sanity* (C. V. Mosby Co., New York, 1988) was a significant landmark in understanding Psychopathic Personalities. Cleckley wrote detailed life stories of people from different walks of life who exhibited characteristics of such personalities. He highlighted that there were very successful businessmen, politicians and even physicians who had some of those characteristics but never found themselves in prisons or psychiatric hospitals because they never got into conflict with the law. They were able to control their impulses and appear "normal" in society.

> *"In these personalities ... a very deep-seated disorder often exists. The true difference between them and the psychopaths who continually go to jails or to psychiatric hospitals is that they keep up a far better and more consistent outward appearance of being normal."*

B. Bursten and Eric Fromm in the 1970's made valuable contributions to the psychoanalytic understanding of psychopathic personalities. Bursten focused on their "manipulative nature" and Fromm on the "exploitative-sadistic" aspects of their personalities. Fromm noted, *"Mental cruelty, the wish to humiliate and to hurt another person's feelings, is probably even more widespread than physical sadism. This type of sadistic attack is much safer for the sadist; after all, no physical force but "only" words have been used. On the other hand, the psychic pain can be as intense or even more so than the physical."*

D. Shapiro in his writings in the1980's agreed with Fromm that sadism plays a significant role in the personality and lifestyle of psychopaths. He feels that psychopaths try to control and manipulate and exploit others by their aggressive behaviours and enjoy humiliating others.

> *"The aims of sadism are, as I said, not only to make the victim suffer but especially to humiliate or degrade him, to make him feel helpless and powerless .... These are aggressive aims of a special kind."*

Otto Kernberg in his writings in the 1980's focused on the narcissistic dimension of Psychopathic Personalities and highlighted how these people are egocentric and selfish because they do not have well-developed super-egos.

> "The resultant absence of a normally integrated super-ego (i.e., of a system of more or less coherent internalized ethical and moral standards) brings about a total dependency of the individual on immediate external clues for the regulation of interpersonal behaviour ...."

Kernberg also highlighted how their anger is turned into hate, making them dangerous individuals for the community.

> "The transformation of pain into rage, and chronic rage into hatred, is a central affective development of these patients. The structural characteristics of hatred imply the relationship between an endangered self and a hateful and hated object that must be controlled, made to suffer in revenge, and ultimately destroyed." ... In the most severe cases of aggressive psychopathy, sexual sadism may become an invitation to murder, making these individuals extremely dangerous."

Robert Hare in the 1980's designed a Psychopathy Checklist based on Cleckley's descriptions, for use as guidelines in mental health and correctional systems to determine the severity of pathology in psychopathic personalities. Such a checklist is one of the attempts by experts to assess these people and protect their families and communities from their anti-social activities.

CLASSIFICATIONS

In the last few decades different international classifications have used different terms to diagnose this special type of personality disorder. In the 1940s, the term "Psychopathic Personality Disorder" was popular, in

1952 the term "Sociopathic Personality Disorder" came into vogue and since 1968 the diagnosis "Personality Disorder- Anti-Social Type" is widely used. These terms try to capture different aspects of these personalities; some highlight the psychological while others the social dimension of the disorder.

Cleckley states, "The diagnostic category 'Personality Disorder' officially includes a wide variety of maladjusted people who cannot by the criteria of psychiatry be classed with the psychotic, the psychoneurotic, or the mentally defective." When the features of psychopathy and anti-social behaviour predominate then the disorder takes the name "Personality Disorder, Antisocial Type."

ASSESSMENT

Among all the psychological tests used to assess personality disorders the one that has become quite popular for psychopathic personalities is the Psychopathy Checklist devised by Hare based on Cleckley's personality profile of psychopathic personalities. In that checklist there are twenty items and the clinician, using data from the interview with the patient, interviews with his relatives and the history provided by other clinicians, scores him on those items. If the characteristic is absent he scores 0, if it is present but in a mild form he scores 1 but if it is strongly present it is scored 2. Thus the person can score up to 40 points. The higher the score the more psychopathic is the individual. Scores higher than 30 are strong indications of the presence of a serious personality disorder with psychopathic traits with poor prognosis. Those twenty characteristics are as follows:

1. Glib and Superficial Charm
2. Grandiose Sense of Self-Worth
3. Need for Stimulation or Proneness to Boredom
4. Pathological Lying
5. Cunning and Manipulativeness
6. Lack of Remorse or Guilt
7. Shallow Affect
8. Callousness and Lack of Empathy

Dr. K. Sohail

9. Parasitic Lifestyle
10. Poor Behavioural Controls
11. Promiscuous Sexual Behaviour
12. Early Behaviour Problems
13. Lack of Realistic, Long-term Goals
14. Impulsivity
15. Irresponsibility
16. Failure to Accept Responsibility for Own Actions
17. Many Short-Term Marital Relationships
18. Juvenile Delinquency
19. Revocation of Conditional Release
20. Criminal Versatility.

Hare's Checklist has been widely used in institutions dealing with psychopathic personalities.

Hare is of the opinion that all psychopaths exhibit anti-social behaviour but all anti-social and criminal acts are not the result of psychopathy.

ETIOLOGICAL FACTORS (causes or origins of disease)

One of the puzzling questions is whether psychopaths are born that way or are made that way by their dysfunctional upbringing. Experts have focused their attention on determining factors that contribute to the development of such a disorder.

GENETIC FACTORS

Genetic studies show that genetic factors are important. Monozygotic (single fertilized ovum) and Dizygotic (two separately fertilized ova) twin studies provide significant evidence that psychopaths inherit some of their psychopathic traits and tendencies.

H. Eysenck reviewed those studies, "Thirteen such studies have been carried out in many different countries (from Norway to Japan, from Germany to the United States), with predicted results in all. For 262 MZ [Monozygotic] twin pairs, the concordance rate was 51.5%; for

375 DZ [Dizygotic] twin pairs, the concordance rate was 20.6% (i.e., less than half). This would suggest heritability for crime of 64%. Studies of Monozygotic twins brought up in separation have also shown good concordance for antisocial criminal conduct (Raine, 1993).

BIOLOGICAL FACTORS

The question of physical differences in the brains of criminals and psychopaths versus those of normal brains is one of the preoccupations of some neurologists and researchers. Some experts feel that psychopathic behaviour is related to the malfunctioning of the frontal lobe of the brain. Raine et al "suggested that deficits localized in the frontal cortex may be related to violence." There is also some evidence that "Persons indulging in various criminal activities tend to be characterized by high testosterone and low Monoamino Oxidase levels."

PSYCHOLOGICAL FACTORS

Most children brought up in normal families develop a sense of right and wrong and then conduct their lives in accordance with their conscience. Eyesenck believed that in normal people conscience is developed by a conditioning process based on the Pavlovian punishment and reward system. He wrote, "Every time we transgress, we are punished by our parents, our teachers, our peers; often when we act in socially approved fashion, we are lauded or rewarded, but in psychopathic personalities such process is defective because of the following three possibilities:

1. The conditioning experiences are missing.
2. The wrong experiences are reinforced.
3. There is overwhelming evidence that anti-social and criminal people show relatively poor conditionability compared with ordinary people."

Historically in the upbringing of children, mothers have played the role of nurturing while fathers played the role of limit setting and disciplining. In the upbringing of many psychopaths, discipline by the

Dr. K. Sohail

father was missing.

"In 1986, of the juveniles incarcerated in the United States for serious crimes, about 70% had been reared without fathers."

(Beck, Kline, and Greenfield 1987).

There were others in whose upbringing fathers played a negative role. Those fathers who had psychopathic tendencies, who were abusive themselves, were poor role models for their children.

Robins did extensive studies of children at risk for psychopathy during the 1960's. He found that "parental pathology predicted psychopathy." Thus, children brought up in homes where they observe violent behaviours are vulnerable to grow up exhibiting anti-social behaviour.

For normal development of personalities and moral codes, children need stable family systems with definite limit setting and clear expectations. Children brought up in chaotic and broken families are vulnerable to develop delinquent behaviours.

Eric Simonsen observed, "The search for the developmental origins of psychopathy has indicated that a significant proportion of children from chaotic and disorganized family environments will develop into criminal, antisocial adults."

Those families that are conservative and strict might cause other emotional problems in their children but such children are protected from psychopathy. Joel Paris wrote,

"Although traditional families have their own difficulties, since their repressive style could make children susceptible to other forms of mental disorder, children raised with clear boundaries and limits are at low risk for psychopathy."

SOCIAL FACTORS

Alongside the family environment, the community also plays a role in instilling values in children. If the school systems and society have strong moral codes and promote supportive social networks, then vulnerable children can be protected. But if other institutions of the community are breaking down alongside the institution of the family, then the children become doubly vulnerable. Paris stated,

"Thus psychopathy is more likely when family breakdown is accompanied by the breakdown of structures outside the family that might have provided community support for children at risk."

CULTURAL FACTORS

Of all the varieties of mental illnesses and emotional problems, personality disorders are the most difficult to study in diverse cultures. Draguns in 1986 wrote,

"It has been argued that unlike the major mental disorders such as depression and schizophrenia, the personality disorders are less likely to have a well-crystallized pan-cultural core."

Different cultures have differing ways of dealing with such people. Some cultures are punitive while others are sympathetic. Some believe in capital punishment while others isolate offenders from the community but let them lead a peaceful life. In the Western world because of the emphasis on human rights, there is strong reaction against capital punishment for psychopaths who have committed murders.

Murphy studied the subject of psychopathy and social reaction in non-industrialized cultures. He focused on the Yoruba of rural Nigeria and the Inuit of Northwest Alaska. He found that Yoruba have a concept, aranakan, which is used for "a person who always goes his own way regardless of others, who is uncooperative, full of malice, and bullheaded." The Inuit also have a concept, kunlangeta, which is used for a person "whose mind knows what to do but does not do it." Such a person repeatedly breaks the rules and is brought to the elders for punishment.

In 1976 Murphy also highlighted that the shamans and healers of those communities were not optimistic about the future of such people, saying, "Historically, the Inuit management strategy for kunlangeta was to invite the sufferer to go hunting, and, when no one was looking, to push him off the ice."

TREATMENT

Most mental health professionals are very reluctant to treat psycho-pathic personalities, as they know that their hard work will not be rewarded. They are aware that psychopaths do not learn from experience and do not change in therapy. They do not develop insights and do not adopt mature and healthy lifestyles like other therapy patients who suffer neuroses and other types of personality problems.

Joel Paris: "Of all the personality disorders, psychopathy offers the most pessimistic prospects for treatment."

INDIVIDUAL THERAPY

Even when therapy is offered, therapists feel that structured therapy with clear expectations might be more beneficial than non-structured therapy. Eyesenck believed that in treating Psychopathic Personalities, behavioural methods might be more effective than psychodynamic approaches. "The large body of empirical study has shown that behavioural approaches based on learning theory are most effective. Traditional psychodynamic and non-directive, client-centered therapies are to be avoided within general samples of offenders." (Andrews, Bonta & Hoge 1990).

Many mental health workers believe that the goal of therapy should not be to change the personality, rather it should be to limit the damage done by these people. Kernberg expressed his views,

> "The prognosis for psychotherapeutic treatment of the antisocial disorder proper is practically zero. The main therapeutic task is to protect the family, the therapist, and society from such a patient, as well as to protect the patient from self-destructiveness."

There is always a danger that because of the psychopath's superficial charm, the therapist may be taken advantage of by the manipulative patient. Kernberg warned therapists, "It is important that the therapist remain firmly in a moral stance without becoming moralistic."

INSTITUTIONAL CARE

Personality Disorders, especially Psychopathic ones are the most difficult to look after in hospitals. They repeatedly test the boundaries and
disobey the rules. The staff find the experience of looking after them
quite frustrating and sometimes even dangerous.

The only method that showed some promise was based on
Maxwell Jones' philosophy. From 1940-1945 Jones and his colleagues
created the basis for the treatment model later to be called the
"Therapeutic Community," with the central realization of the strength of
peer group support in large-group situations and the value of fellow
patients in passing on the culture and philosophy of treatment to newly
admitted individuals.

The approach was used in Henderson Hospital in England. By
using that method, "The unit's treatment approach moved away from
an authoritarian, hierarchical style to one that was more collaborative
and democratic. Patients were expected to take an active part both in
their own treatment and that of other patients."

In the Therapeutic Community philosophy, patients play an active
role in their treatment which is why they are called "residents" rather
than "patients" to avoid passive connotations of the later term. In such
programs the focus is more on group therapies rather than individual
counseling. Residents are in active group therapies for a minimum of 25
hours each week.

Henderson Hospital showed very positive results and proved that
the Therapeutic Community approach to personality disorders could
be quite effective if the residents took part in the program faithfully and
were discharged only after the treatment team was satisfied with their
progress. Such an approach has been a breakthrough in treating personality disorders. Research workers focusing on the results of
Henderson Hospital were impressed by their results.

*"It was demonstrated that 41% of admitted patients were free of
reconviction or readmission at a three year follow up, compared with only 23% of the non-admitted group. Five-year
follow-up rates were 36% and 19%, respectively. The study also
demonstrated that outcome improved with length of stay in*

treatment, with 62% of those admitted for over six months and 71% of those who stayed over nine months being free of reconviction or readmission at a three-year follow-up." (Copas, O'Brien, Roberts & Whitley 1984).

The philosophy and practice of the Therapeutic Community approach has been a major breakthrough in looking after personality disorders, especially psychopaths. Those prisons that have a progressive attitude are adopting a therapeutic philosophy and are called Therapeutic Prisons. They are offering a ray of hope in an area where most people feel very frustrated and pessimistic. Therapeutic Prisons might be of value to communities, mental health professionals and government agencies worldwide.

It is clear from the above discussion that problems created by psychopathic personalities are a concern for all segments of society. Cleckley had written in 1941,

"These people called psychopaths present a problem which must be better understood by lawyers, social workers, schoolteachers, and by the general public if any satisfactory way of dealing with them is to be worked out."

I strongly believe that the human beings we label as psychopaths and criminals are part of us. We need to develop a humanistic, rather than a punitive approach. Rather than eliminating them through capital punishment, we need to accept them as part of our communities and work hard on finding solutions to their problems. We are all part of the same community. In 1994, Judge Charles Gill stated,

"While political leaders can now feel comfortable calling for draconian measures to punish the citizens they describe as 'predators', 'monsters'and 'punks', none has the true courage and vision to solve the problem.

"You might ask our political leaders, 'Where do these monsters, predators and punks come from? Did they parachute from another country? Did they emerge from a spaceship from another planet?' We know three things about these hated citizens. One, they were all born in American hospitals; two, they

were all educated in American schools; and three, they were all reared by American adults. It is a rare predator indeed who has had a successful childhood."

⌘ 20 Javed Iqbal and Modern Serial Killers

While I was exploring the criminal dimension of Javed Iqbal's life, and studying his diaries, I was wondering about the similarities and differences between his story and the stories of others who confessed to multiple murders.

BIZARRE EXPLANATIONS

The first thing that struck me was that many serial killers have given bizarre reasons for their actions. The explanations they offer for their actions are quite strange and surrealistic and they keep on changing their story as time passes because they do not fully understand their own motives. Javed Iqbal emphasized that his stay in the hospital was so traumatic for his mother that she got sick and died; he blamed his enemies for his mother's death and promised to himself that he would kill one hundred children so that their mothers suffer the same way as his mother.

Lucian Staniak, from Poland who had confessed to 20 murders, claimed that he killed women out of revenge. His parents and sister were killed in a car accident by a woman driver; so he attacked any woman who looked like that woman. He used to send letters and his black poetry to the media. Some of his famous lines are: "There is no happiness without tears, no life without death. Beware, I will give you cause to weep," and "I picked a juicy flower in Olsztyn and I shall do it again somewhere else, for there is no holiday without a funeral."

Peter Kurten, a serial killer from Germany used to say that he derived sexual pleasure from watching the blood flow.

MAKING A POINT

Most serial killers and mass murderers try to make a point. Sometimes they do it by writing their diaries and confessions and sometimes by giving extensive interviews to police, media and mental health professionals.

Clifford Olsen, from British Columbia who pled guilty to eleven counts of murder in 1982 and was sentenced to eleven concurrent life sentences, has been writing his philosophy for years on topics ranging from immortality to love.

Panzman while waiting for his execution wrote, "I don't believe in man, God nor Devil. I hate the whole damned race including myself ... I have consistently followed one idea through all my life. I preyed upon the weak, the harmless and unsuspecting. The lesson I was taught by others: might makes right."

Those serial killers are neither intellectuals nor philosophers and they do not have a well-organized conceptual framework yet they like to make a statement, a statement that is personal and political at the same time. Ironically, to make that statement they use a gun more than a pen. I sometimes wonder, if they could have used the pen better, they might not have needed to rely on the gun.

Javed Iqbal wanted to be a journalist and reform society, but when he could not succeed in making a name in a creative way, he chose the destructive route.

CONTRADICTIONS

It is not uncommon to see some strange contradictions in the life styles of serial killers and mass murderers, which reflect incongruent aspects of their personalities. Sometimes they are very generous, other times very miserly. In some ways they are very loving, in other ways very cruel. Charles Starkweather was one such example. He hated people but loved nature. He killed human beings but gave donations to animal welfare organizations.

Sometimes their personalities and lifestyles need extensive study to find deeper meaning in their superficially meaningless acts.

Javed Iqbal, on one hand, mapped out a detailed plan to kill young people in his diary, but on the other hand insisted in the interview that he loved children.

MOTIVATION

Although each serial killer and mass murderer has a unique set of motives, there are some factors that are common to many of them.

The most common factor is revenge They are very angry and resentful and finally their hurt turns into revenge. The interesting thing about this revenge is that it is generalized. Rather than killing the individuals who hurt them they generalize it to that individual's ethnic, racial, religious or socio-economic group. They fantasize about destroying that segment of the society as they see it as evil and oppressive.

Edmund Kemper III wanted to hurt rich people, members of the upper class, as he believed he suffered from being poor. Mark Essex wanted to kill white people, as he believed he had suffered racial discrimination in the United States Navy due to his being black. James Huberty targeted Hispanic people, shooting people indiscriminately in a McDonald's restaurant in California. He blamed them for his unemployment and suffering.

Javed Iqbal in his diaries targets Pathans. He believed that the employee who tried to kill him was a Pathan. Reading the police reports it becomes evident that the people who had him charged with sodomy the first time in 1990 were also Pathans. So Javed Iqbal tried to justify his actions as taking revenge on that tribal group.

Hatred towards women seems a common theme with many serial killers. Many killers like Albert Desalvo and Theodore Bundy sexually abused women, used them as objects of lust and then destroyed them. It appears that their anger and hatred towards women was very deep rooted.

PROTEST AGAINST MEDIOCRITY

Many serial killers and mass murderers realize quite early in life that their dreams might be lofty but they themselves are basically mediocre and will never amount to anything. They keep on hoping and dreaming, and one day when they realize that they are doomed never to make a mark in their lives by regular means, they take drastic measures to be something and somebody.

DEHUMANIZATION

Serial killers reach a stage in their lives when they lose all regard for other human beings and all respect for humanity. For them, whether their victims are rich or poor, men or women, children or elderly, they are objects of sexual and aggressive lust and they want to destroy them indiscriminately. They do not even know these people personally. For them, a human being becomes an abstraction, a symbol, a metaphor. They kill for the sake of killing. They turn killing into a destructive art and their own hearts into stones.

> *"Once that you've decided on a killing*
> *First you make a stone of your heart*
> *And if you find that your hands are still willing*
> *You can turn murder into art.*
> *("Synchronicity" by The Police, 1983)"*

Javed Iqbal in his diaries wrote, "*... our hearts have turned into stones.*"

CELEBRITY STATUS

Many serial killers and mass murderers yearn to achieve celebrity status. They do not hesitate to contact the national media — newspapers, radio and television. For a chance at fame, they make false confessions and confuse police and public alike. For them it becomes a big game. They want to go all the way, to be remembered in history.

Many of them hold regular meetings in prison with the media and their biographers, to discuss plans for publication of their books and for making documentaries and feature films of their lives.

Michael McGray claimed to have committed a dozen murders across Canada in the last fifteen years but even his lawyer wondered how much of it is true and how much is fiction.

Peter Worthington, a Toronto journalist, questions whether many of the confessions from serial killers might be more of a reflection of "mass deception" than "mass murder" and Javed Iqbal may not be an exception.

MESSIAH COMPLEX

Some serial killers and mass murderers genuinely believe that they are "The Chosen Ones". They believe they have a profound message and only if people embraced that message, it could liberate them from oppressive groups and systems and help them on the path of growth, maturity and evolution. Essex believed he was a Black Messiah, the chosen one, a Messiah who carried a rifle, not a cross.

But there is always a paradox. They choose the path of destruction to reach the destination of peace and nirvana. That is why it is not uncommon for communities to perceive such personalities as evil and go to extremes to punish, persecute and penalize them. In their eyes they are the chosen ones to be made a " horrible example" for generations to come.

Javed Iqbal also believes that when he was a child, a saint had announced that he was *The Chosen One* to save and heal his people and that if someone broke his heart, then the blessing would turn into a curse and the whole family and community would suffer. Javed Iqbal is convinced that the saint's prediction is coming true.

⌛ 21 *The Dark Side of Humanity*

"Man is the only species that is a mass murderer,
the only misfit in his own society. Why should this be so?"
— N. Tinbergen

While exploring the personalities, lifestyles and social environments of serial killers and mass murderers and reading their biographies I realized that I was peering into the darkest corners of human nature. I found myself facing the simple but profound philosophical question:

What is human nature?

To answer this question satisfactorily, I found lay people as well as "experts" equally lost. They have a hard time explaining the most irrational acts in a rational way.

As far as lay people are concerned, some believe human beings are basically bad, evil, sinful and selfish and are not surprised at all to see the killings and murders committed by human beings as they believe it is part of their nature.

There are others who believe human beings are basically good, kind, compassionate, selfless and altruistic and blame the negative on the faulty upbringing and destructive social environment. They think negative environments turn angels into devils. They do not believe anyone is a born killer.

And then there are those who believe that human nature is basically neutral. It is like a blank sheet. Human beings have the same potential to become angels or devils, saints or sinners, prophets or serial killers. They see human babies as dough that can be molded into a hundred different forms.

When I studied the views of experts, whether they were biologists, psychologists, sociologists or anthropologists, I was reminded of those philosophers who were trying to comprehend an elephant in a dark room and each one described the elephant depending upon the part of the elephant they were touching. Their descriptions were more reflection of their perception than the reality.

The first philosopher I came across was Konrad Lorenz (1903-1989) of Austria. He believed that aggression is a part of human nature that we share with our animal ancestors. Sooner or later the aggressive energy builds and then is released depending on the stimulus and environment. There are times aggression is expressed even when there is no provocation because it is constantly flowing.

"...human aggressiveness is an instinct fed by an ever-flowing fountain of energy, and not necessarily the result of a reaction to other stimuli. Lorenz holds that energy specific for an instinctive act accumulates continuously in the neural centres related to that behavioural pattern, and if energy has been accumu-

lated an explosion is likely to occur even without the presence
of a stimulus .... Man, he says, creates political parties in order
to find stimuli for the release of dammed-up energy, rather than
political parties being the cause of aggression." (Ref. 1 p. 17)

I always felt that Lorenz saw people more as animals than humans and
did not fully appreciate that human nature is not as fixed as the nature
of fish, birds and animals. Rabbits always eat grass, never meat and
lions always eat meat and never grass; but human beings can eat meat
or remain vegetarian depending upon their choices because of intrinsic
flexibility of their nature. They have a duality, a duality of being angel or
devil, saint or sinner as part of their nature.

The second philosopher was Sigmund Freud, founder of psycho-
analysis, who believed that human beings have life and death instincts
and that the death instinct makes people destructive whether towards
themselves or others. Freud had quite a sophisticated conceptual
framework to explain the dynamics of those instincts.

"Freud recognized that life is not ruled by two egotistic drives,
one for food, the other for sex, but by two passions—love and
destruction—that do not serve physiological survival in the
same sense that hunger and sexuality do. Still bound by his the-
oretical premises, however, he called them 'life instinct' and
'death instinct' and thereby gave human destructiveness its
dignity as one of two fundamental passions in man"

Freud's concepts of conscious, preconscious, unconscious and defense
mechanisms explained many aspects of human personality and motivation that could not be explained by descriptive psychology before.
Freud was courageous enough to explore some dark aspects of human
nature and offer insights.

In spite of his awareness of personal dynamics he did not fully
incorporate many social and cultural factors in his theory that many
sociologists and anthropologists have since recognized.

The third philosopher studied was B.F. Skinner. He offered scientific explanations for human behaviors. He believed children can be

D r .   K .   S o h a i l

trained to behave well or badly depending what their families and schools and communities consider good or bad. He called that process "Operant Conditioning".

> "Skinner's 'psychology' is the science of the engineering of behavior; its aim is to find the right reinforcements in order to produce a desired behavior." (Ref. 1 p. 34)

I found Skinner's theory too mechanical. I felt Skinner saw human beings as sophisticated machines or robots that can be programmed. It seemed as if Skinner did not give full credit to human intentions and motivations. He did not address the process of evolution of values.

After reading Lorenz, Freud and Skinner, I moved on to Eric Fromm, Abraham Maslow and Richard Bucke. Their theories seemed to be more comprehensive and opened new doors of awareness. Eric Fromm in his book, *The Anatomy of Human Destructiveness*, puts forward the theory that there are different forms of aggression and we have to understand their dynamics differently. He highlights that human personality and character is the main stage of human drama where instincts, behaviors and social factors interact with each other. He stresses the point that until we fully comprehend the human character, we will not be able to put the pieces of puzzle together. After we grasp the character then we can understand the complex motivations of human beings. He differentiates *Benign* Aggression that we share with animals which is of a defensive nature and is needed for our survival, from *Malignant* Aggression that is purely human and not found in animals. This Malignant Aggression is the cause of killing for the sake of killing, murder for the sake of murder and cruelty for the sake of cruelty.

> "We must distinguish in man two entirely different kinds of aggression. The first, which he shares with all animals is phylogenetically programmed impulse to attack (or to flee) when vital interests are threatened. This defensive "benign" aggression is in the service of the survival of the individual and the species, is biologically adaptive, and ceases when the threat has ceased to exist. The other type, "malignant" aggression,

i.e., destructiveness and cruelty, is specific to the human species and virtually absent in most mammals; it is not phylogenetically programmed and not biologically adaptive; it has no purpose, and its satisfaction is lustful." (Ref. 1 p. 4)

Some people develop sadomasochistic personalities and adopt a lifestyle in which they control and destroy others and finally themselves. That is where humans act worse than animals and have regressed rather than evolved. Unfortunately the higher human beings can fly, the lower they can fall.

Abraham Maslow in his book *Motivation and Personality* (HarperCollins, New York, 1970) highlights how different people are motivated by different needs depending upon where they are in their personal growth and maturity. Maslow offered a concept of hierarchy of needs. At the lower level are people who are motivated by their survival needs. For them food and shelter are the cornerstones of their lives while on the other extreme are people who are motivated by their self-actualizing needs. They are highly evolved. Maslow broadened the horizons of human nature and encouraged us to include the highly evolved people, alongside the sick and the average people to understand the range of human nature.

While Maslow highlighted the evolution of human personality and character in an individual's life, Richard Bucke focused on the evolution of the whole species. He even went further. In his book *Cosmic Consciousness* (Ref. 2) he shares his theory that life has gone through three stages of consciousness.

The first stage was *Simple Consciousness*. That is the stage where fish and birds and animals live.

The second stage was *Self Consciousness*. When animals developed self-consciousness they became human and developed language and religion and art with their evolved imagination.

The third stage is *Cosmic Consciousness*. Only a few in every century develop that level of consciousness. Bucke believed that Buddha and Christ and Walt Whitman were some of those over the centuries who had developed Cosmic Consciousness. He believed that gradually more and more people will develop Cosmic Consciousness.

D r .   K .   S o h a i l

"Our ancestry of self consciousness dates back to the first true man. Thousands of years must have elapsed between its first appearance and its universality, just as thousands of years are now passing between the first cases of cosmic consciousness and its universality." (Ref.1 p.47)

Bucke also highlights that being fully human means to develop not only language and abstract thought, but also moral sense which:

"...includes many faculties, such as conscience, the abstract sense of right and wrong, sexual love as distinguished from sexual desire or instinct, parental and filial love as distinguished from the corresponding instincts... love of our fellow men as such, love of the beautiful, awe, reverence, sense of duty and responsibility, sympathy, compassion, faith."

Bucke believes that since moral sense is only a few thousand years old in the evolution of mankind, it has not become universal. He compares it with colour sense. The way we have many among us, those who are colour blind — there are also many who do not have a well developed moral sense.

"...the proportion of the adults who have little or no, or an undeveloped, moral nature is far greater than of those who have little or no, or undeveloped color sense."

Those who never develop moral sense are known as sociopaths and psychopaths.

Bucke believed that the way Self Consciousness has become universal in human adults, similarly after thousands of years of evolution, moral sense and Cosmic Consciousness will also become universal and we will see more saints and mystics and artists and scientists and philosophers in human species than serial killers and mass murderers.

I only hope that in the meanwhile we do not commit collective suicide or collective murder because we have reached a stage in human evolution where we can commit such a mass murder that we can kill the whole species and other species as well. I hope that we can travel on the path of human evolution and become fully human, the enlightened beings. I hope we as human beings become the species that is the chosen one to embrace Cosmic Consciousness and become the enlightened species.

Ref. 1 - *Anatomy of Human Destructiveness*, Eric Fromm.

Ref. 2 - *Cosmic Consciousness*, R. Bucke, Penguin Books, USA, 1969.

⌛ 22 *Excerpts from the Diaries of Javed Iqbal*

"OUR HEARTS HAVE TURNED TO STONES"
1999

There was a time I used to live happily in Fatehgarh. I had a good business. I used to run two video game stores and earn 500-700 rupees a day. Life was comfortable and enjoyable. I had close friends like Yaseen and Naseem Murshad whom I knew for the last twenty years. We used to spend weekends together and have a good time. I had a number of employees including Zafar, Sajid, Arbab and Abdur Rahman who used to look after us.

And then I decided to sell my house and move somewhere else because I was not very happy with my neighbours who were very selfish and unreasonable. On the 15th of September [1998] I went to Yadgar-e-Pakistan with Arbab as all the other employees had gone on holidays. Over there I met a dark-coloured teenager. I offered him a job and he agreed. As we were coming home, passing close to Do Moria Pul [Do Moria Bridge], we met another young boy. I offered him a job and he came with us too. The first teenager was from Narowaal and the second from Kohat.

I had put an ad in the newspaper for the 17th and 20th of September to sell my house. On the 17th, a number of people came to see the house. I made a deal with a major. He promised to give me two lakh [two hundred] rupees in two days and then three lakh and forty thousand in 15-20 days. I agreed. After the major left, my old employee

Yaseen and two new employees asked me if the deal was done and I said, "Yes". After that conversation I left. That night I slept upstairs and Arbab and the two new employees slept downstairs. I turned off the air conditioner before I went to bed. I had awoken quite early that morning so I fell asleep right away.

On the 8th of October [1998] when I regained my consciousness, I was lying in my mother's house. Mom told me that I was sick and that I had experienced a major crisis. I found out that on the night of the 17th of September, I and my child Arbab were killed. I was unconscious in the General Hospital for 22 days. They had tried to kill me when I was asleep in my home in Fatehgarh. I found out that in the morning when the neighbours heard Arbab crying they came to the door. My employee from Kohat opened the door. The neighbours came in upstairs and found me soaked in blood. I was unconscious. I was badly bruised and hurt and my face was quite swollen. Neighbours called the police and took me to the hospital. My employees said that some visitors came and beat me up but that is not true. The reality is that at night my employees from Narowaal and Kohat tried to sexually abuse Arbab and he started to scream. After molesting him, they hit him on the head and then came and beat me up badly with a gun. After that they took my keys and stole 8000 rupees [about $300.00 Canadian]. They were looking for 2 lakh rupees.

When the neighbours came, the employee of Narowaal had disappeared but they caught the employee from Kohat with 8000 rupees and handed him over to the police. The police officer liked that young Pathan, so rather than charging him, gave him a job in his own house. He still lives with that officer. The officer provided refuge to a criminal. The police ruined my case and accused me of molesting young Arbab. My family members were told lies by the police. They paid Arbab's parents 10,000 rupees and sent him to his village. Arbab was also unconscious in the hospital for ten days. I was utterly disappointed in the role of the police in this case. They were the same police that I tried to help for the last twelve years. What they did to me was character assassination.

With the grace of God I regained consciousness after 22 days. I sold my house, my car and my expensive furniture. I had four operations and stayed in the hospital for months. During that time the only person who stayed with me and supported me was my mother.

After selling my house in Fatehgarh, I rented a house on Ravi Road and started living there. Since my mother was getting weak and sick, she arranged the marriage of my sister with my employee Iqbal. When my friends heard the news of the marriage they came to see me. One of them was Nasim, whom I have known for the last twenty years, and I call him Murshad. Our friendship had been great and on the weekends we used to spend the whole day together. When Murshad saw my condition, he became quite upset. He told me that while investigating my case, the police had been bothering my friends. That was the reason Murshad had disappeared from the scene. He was worried that the police might hurt him.

In spite of the doctor's care, my condition did not improve. I was so limited I could hardly walk. I had spent thousands of rupees, but my health had not improved. I asked Murshad Naseem if he would take my remaining 2-3 lakh rupees and invest it in the business on my behalf but he did not agree. He was worried that it would tie up my money and I would not be able to use it for my operations if I needed it.

One day Murshad came and I told him that I did not want to live anymore. I could go to Yadgar-e-Pakistan and find my murderer because that was where I had met him the first time. He told me, "All your life you tried to help your employees but they were never faithful to you. Before you die you should get rid of them too because they tried to kill you." His words stuck in my mind. I liked the idea of getting rid of them, killing them. I was aware that death was following me. I asked Murshad to suggest a plan to kill as many as possible because they tried to kill me, the innocent one. They made my life miserable. I did not want to die alone. I wanted to take them with me, those who hurt me. Murshad and I thought and thought for days but could not come up with a plan that could kill a lot of people in a short time.

Finally one day Murshad found a solution to our dilemma. He suggested that we could dissolve the dead bodies in acid and then throw them into a sewage gutter. We decided to buy chemical cans and plastic drums. We planned to bring teenagers from Yadgar-e-Pakistan who had run away from home, offer them jobs and then kill them, cut their dead bodies into pieces, dissolve them in acid and then throw

Dr. K. Sohail

them into the gutter. The problem was who would buy the acid and who would throw away the dissolved dead bodies into the gutter. I took my sixteen-year old employee Sabir Hassain into my confidence, shared the plan, and asked him to help us. He agreed. So we stated to put our plan into action on the 19th of June [1999]. During the whole project I used different people for different actions as I was not even able to go to the washroom by myself. I was so weak and disabled that I could not kill teenagers, cut them into pieces, put those pieces in acid drums and then drain the dissolved bodies into the gutter. I needed other people to help me put the plan into action. I asked different people to get me acid without telling them what I was using it for.

February 20th. I sold the house in Fatehgurh today. Iqbal and his three younger brothers helped me move. I slept in the new house for the first time. Mom stayed with me tonight.

February 22nd. I saw Dr. Yaqoob Beg today. He did the check up and suggested surgery.

February 24th. Mom, Iqbal and my.employee Sabir Hussain went with me to the Gulberg Hospital so that I could have the operation.

February 25th. I had the operation today. A lot of relatives and friends came to see me. Even my daughter and wife Nazli came to see me this evening and brought lots of flowers.

March 9th. Today we went to the Holy shrine of Mian Ji. Mom, Shahzad and Sajid joined me too. I prayed all night long and asked for forgiveness of my sins. My mom prayed too. We will stay with her for a few days.

March 15th. After staying at the shrine for a few days, today we will go back home to Ravi Road. I have not been feeling very well.

March 16th. After offering the sacrifice we left the shrine last night. Mom went to my sister Nunny's place and Shahzad and Sajid came with me.

March 18th. Murshad Nasim came today. He stayed for a while and then left.

March 22nd. Today Sajid met Naeem somewhere and brought him home. I asked him to stay and gave him some clothes. He used to work for me for two months. I had not seen him for a few months. He looked sad when he saw my miserable condition.

March 23rd.   While talking to Naeem, I made a plan to visit the shrine of Data Darbar. With the grace of God I will go there regularly to pray.

March 26th.   Azhar came back to work with me. He lives in Shad Bagh. He joined my other employees Sabir, Sajid and Naeem.

March 27th.   I went to the shrine of Data Darbar with Naeem and Shahzad. I prayed all night long.

March 29th.   I spent the night at the shrine of Data Darbar. Shahzad and Naeem were with me.

March 30th.   We went to Data Darbar shrine. Spent the night there and prayed.

March 30th.   Baba Yaseen came to see how I was doing. He has to get his hernia operation done. I offered to pay for all the expenses of the operation. He was quite pleased to hear that.

April 1st.   I have been going to Data Darbar on a regular basis to pray.

May 2nd.   Nasim Murshad came today and we discussed our plan. He shared the plan with Baba Yaseen and asked him to help me. He agreed.

May 3rd.   Zafar came today. I told him I want to take revenge. He agreed with me and told me it was my right as I was wronged. His support boosted my confidence.

May 7th.   I made an offer to Zafar to pay him 2500 rupees a month to help me put my plan into action. I gave him 5000 rupees to buy snacks for the teenagers we will bring from Yadgar-e-Pakistan to kill.

June 7th.   My friends Maulvi Riaz and Ashiq Hussain Bhatti came to see me. I was glad to see them. They were my good friends in Fatehgarh. Ashiq Hussain had borrowed a fridge, sofa, chairs and folding bed when he needed

	them. He had also reciprocated my affection many times.
June 9th.	Today Zafar and Sabir went to Sajid's house to invite him back. Sajid's mother told them that he was not home. They knew she was lying so they waited outside the house and he came out after a couple of hours. Sajid had run away with 2900 rupees. He was told that he was forgiven by me so he came back. Later on Zafar told me that his mother had received 5000 rupees from a hotel and she wanted him to leave us and work in that hotel. I told him he was free to choose, so he left.
June 13th.	Today Nasir Shaikh came to see me. Nasim Murshad had given him my address. He was really upset to see my terrible condition. I told him that Murshad and I have planned to end the world. He said it was the right thing to do. He was quite thrilled with our plan.
June 14th.	I discussed with Nasir if he would invest some of my money in his Zeeshan Pipe Store in Ram Street No.3. He said he was discussing business with his friends. He will get back to me in a few days.
June 15th.	Although Zafar left us, he still comes regularly and sleeps here. He left because his mom asked him to, but he is still attached to us. I am quite pleased with his behaviour. I keep on giving him his allowance.
June 16th.	My brother-in-law Goshi Nadeem, and Azeem Qureshi, came to see me. They also brought my daughter's gift, a bouquet of flowers. I was quite pleased to receive them. They did not stay long.
June 17th.	Nasim Murshad came today and returned 5000 out of 10,000 rupees that he had borrowed from me.
June 19th.	Today I cashed a 10,000 rupee cheque. I bought two drums and eight cans of acid. I told the boys that my friend has a factory in Rana Town and I am investing in his business. I told them that we would be melting metallic rods in acid.
June 20th.	Nasim Murshad came today. We went to Yadgar-e-Pakistan and brought a 15-year-old boy, Yasir, from

The Myth of the Chosen One

Hafiz-abad. After arriving home, we sent other boys out to do some work. When we gave Yasir four sleeping pills, he fell asleep. Then we put Sulphuric acid in a bottle, added cyanide, put a mask on Yasir's face, connected it with a rubber pipe and let him inhale the gas fumes from the poisonous acid. After a few breaths, Yasir was dead. Nasim's experiment was 100 percent successful. Then Sabir and I put the dead body in the drum and Nasim and Sabir put two cans of acid in the drum and covered it. This was our first murder. Nasim stayed till the evening. We saw the dead body in the drum a few times. The dead body was rotting and melting but because of the acid there was no bad odour.

The next evening Nasim came again. We sent the boys to Yadgar and peeped into the drum. The dead body had dissolved in the acid. A few pieces were left. We put them in a bucket of acid and they all were dissolved by the morning. The experiment was successful. We were all very happy.

The next day we went to the shrine of Data Darbar to get another boy but we were not successful. Nasim wanted a Pathan boy but we did not find any. Nasim left in the evening. I was happy that I could kill an innocent boy without the help of the police. I am now able to take revenge for my own murder. Before I leave this world, I want many others to leave before me.

June 24th.   Today Maulvi Riaz and Ashiq Hussain came to see me. Ashiq Hussain was the friend who took me and young Arbab to the hospital the day we were killed. He also looked after us in the hospital. I owe him a lot. I told them the whole story of my taking revenge and showed him the drums of acid and the dead body in it. I shared with them that Nasim Murshad was helping me. They were quite happy seeing me do all that.

June 25th.   Today I made a big mistake. I shared my plan with Haji

Shahid who is my cousin and brother-in-law. After telling the details I realized my mistake and decided to keep my mouth shut, otherwise the news will leak before I complete my project.

June 26th. Zafar Iqbal brought a 15-year-old boy from Mevamundi. He was fair coloured and belonged to a village near Peshawar. I sent the other boys out. Zafar gave him five sleeping pills mixed in juice. When he fell asleep we let him inhale poisonous gas and he died within a short time. We put his dead body into drum number 2 and put 2 cans of acid in it. I gave Zafar 500 rupees as a reward. The second murder was successful. This time Sabir helped Zafar.

June 27th. Nobody even Murshad came to visit me on Sunday.

June 28th. Shaikh Nasir came today. I showed him the drums and told him that a dead body dissolves in one day. When I told him the details, he was very happy. He encouraged me. Then he told me that he wants to get a few people killed. He promised to come again. He wanted to see a murder. I told him that he could bring young boys who had run away from home and kill them here. He was happy to hear that and left.

June 29th. Our lovely boy Naeem who was 14 was very beautiful. He came to work with us three months ago but he used to disappear at night. I was fed up with him. He was quite clever. I got concerned as he had some idea of our activities. Murshad Nasim came today. I consulted him about Naeem. He suggested we should not take any risk and get rid of him right away. I felt sad when I gave permission to kill him. At seven o'clock he was given 9 sleeping pills and then we let him inhale poisonous gas. He was our third murder. My heart cried for him. I peeped into the drum many times to see his dead body melt and dissolve.

Naeem's address that he had given me was 74 Chuck, house number 40, street Machi Pura, Cheecha Watni.

In my project Naseem, Zafar and Sabir are helping me a lot. Yaseen had promised to help us but he did not come. He has not been well. He's worried about his hernia operation.

July 1st.
Murshad Nasim did not come today. Sabir was all alone. He went to Yadgar and brought an eighteen year old boy who was from Khanewal. We offered him a milkshake which six tablets of Valium 10 mixed in it. After he fell asleep, we put a mask on his face and he inhaled poisonous gas. He was soon unconscious. His eyes rolled. Sabir and I put him in the drum with great difficulty. Sabir put acid in the drum. So we killed the fourth person. I did not even ask his name because Sabir gave him Valium before I could properly talk to him. I did not care what his name was.

July 3rd.
At seven in the evening Mom, Saeed and my nephew [sister's son] Sohail came. Mom brought two suits for me. I was quite touched by my mother's affection. Mom stayed for a short time and left. I wondered how would my mom cope when I die. That thought upset me.

July 5th.
Today Sabir brought a fat boy who had a dark complexion but still had beautiful features. His name was Sharif and he belonged to Bhaipharu. When I asked his home address, he was evasive. He spent the night with us. Before he went to sleep, Sabir gave him six tablets of Valium 10. Since there were two other boys working with us, we did not get time and privacy to kill him. In the morning at six we got rid of him. We were hardly finished with our job when my nephew (sister's son) Shehzad came to inform us that my mom had become quite sick. She had a heart attack and was admitted to the hospital. I went to the hospital right away. Mom was in bad shape. Mom's condition had deteriorated because she always worried about me. My murderers had not only killed me they made my mother suffer too. Seeing my pathetic condition she

had become a heart patient. Last time when she came to visit me, I could hardly walk. My murderers are responsible for my mom's ill health. If my mom has suffered so much, I will make sure others' mothers suffer too. If I am in pain, I will make sure others are in pain too. I had taken pity on poor employees and tried to help them financially but they tried to kill me. If those poor people could become cruel then I can take revenge too before I die. With the grace of God I will kill dozens of them.

July 9th.
Doctors are trying their best to keep my mom alive with the help of machines. I take a rickshaw and visit my mom every day. I stay in the hospital from morning to evening. My brothers, sisters and sisters-in-law come and spend some time with my mom in the hospital. From the 5th of July I have been spending time there. I told Iqbal, who I have helped since his childhood, that I am spending the last days of my life. I told him that I am taking revenge of my murderers. When he asked the details I laughed it off.

July 12th.
Got worried hearing that Mom's condition is deteriorating. I asked Zafar to get another boy. He got a boy Imran who belonged to Multan. He was 14 or 15. Zafar and I finished him off and put him in the second drum. The dark acid present in the first drum was thrown in the latrine. Then we put fresh acid in the drum. It was our sixth murder.

July 13th.
Today Zafar and Sabir killed another boy Hanif who was from Faisal-abad. I am so hurt about my mother's illness that I have given the boys free reign. Hanif was 14 years old. Nasir came to visit today. I shared the details with him and showed him the drums. He was quite pleased. He left after a few hours.

July 14th.
Today Zafar and Sabir finished off another boy from Multan. His name was Akhtar and he was 15 years old. Since my mother is dying I have given boys all the

freedom to kill the way they want. My mother is dying because of the cruelties of my murderers. I go to the hospital late or return after a short time. I do not stay there long.

July 15th.   Today Nasim Murshad came and brought a 16-year-old boy with him. He was from Shaikhupura. He had already given him six sleeping pills on the way. As soon as he got home, he fell asleep and then with the help of a gas mask died. In the rush, I did not even write down his name. Sabir was the only one at home. Nasim Murshad and Sabir did the work together. It was our ninth murder.

July 16th.   Today Zafar brought a young boy from Havaili Lakha. His name was Majid. Zafar and Sabir finished his work together. They poured the drums in the latrine and flushed it with water in the buckets. Then they put Majid in the drum and poured acid in it.

Mom is still in critical condition lying in the emergency ward. When I see my mother's condition, I feel like destroying the whole city. I have given the boys permission to do whatever they want. From the 13th to 16th, we have murdered one boy every day. It takes two days for the dead body to dissolve.

Then we drain the acid into the toilet. This is part of my revenge. I want their mothers to suffer like my mother suffered and lead a miserable life like mine.

July 19th.   Zafar has not been coming since 16th of July. I am quite worried. Sajid does not know all the details. I have told him that I get these chemicals for the sake of my friend, who takes it away every morning and then brings the empty cans back. Sajid takes drugs, uses Chars [marijuana] and gets up late in the morning. So far he has believed my explanation and has brought acid regularly. Sometimes Nasim Murshad and Zafar buy it too.

July 20th.   Today Nasim Murshad brought Shehzad Chitta with him. I did so many favours to this boy but he always remained my enemy. Nasim gave him Chars and then 4 Valium tablets in his juice. When Nasim got rid of him, I thanked him.

July 21st.   Today I told Zafar and Sabir that the time has come that we need to speed up our work so that I can take the final revenge of all the sufferings that I had to face in the past.

Something very strange happened today. At 10 pm, my old friends Maulvi Riaz, Ashiq and Bhatti came with a suitcase in their pickup truck. They asked me to send my boys out. When I sent the boys to Yadgar they showed me the dead body of a 50 to 55-year-old man that they had brought. The body looked fresh, as it had not become stiff. They had strangled him with a rope. They asked me to do something with the dead body. I opened the room with the drum. They put the dead body in the drum and put acid in it. They told me that he was their enemy and that is why they had killed him. They were very thankful. In this way I returned their favours. They left after a short time.

July 22nd.   Sabir and Zafar brought three boys today and finished them all in their sleep. The first one was Imran who was chubby and belonged to Sialkot. He was fair coloured and looked healthy. The second one was Naimat who did not share his address with us. The third one was a Pathan from Muzaffarabad. He refused to tell us his name and address. This was the first time we killed three boys in one day and put them in our drums. Our confidence is high now. We are getting good at trapping these boys who have run away from home.

July 23rd.   Zafar brought a boy from Sabzi-mandi, Lahore. I was against killing someone local but Zafar convinced me that nobody had seen him bringing the boy. He had run away from home. His name was Shaukat and he was 14. He was killed and thrown in a drum full of acid. Today the count reached 15. This is a great success especially for a disabled man like me who can hardly walk. I can not even lift dead bodies. My boys have helped me a lot. I could not do all that without their support.

July 25th. Our success has boosted our confidence. We have discovered that in our drums we can put three dead bodies at a time. Two cans of acid does the trick. This is my way of getting the ultimate revenge from the world.

July 26th. Mom died today. It is hell for me. Mom was everything for me. My worries killed my mom. My murderers by trying to kill me also killed my mother. I will take revenge by making hundreds of other mothers suffer. With the help of God I will succeed in my plan. I tried to help poor and homeless boys but they tried to kill me. One of them was caught but the police officer protected him by giving him refuge in his own house. After the news of my killings gets public I will see how that officer protects himself. I do not have any hope in people or police to do justice.

After my mom's funeral I told my brothers that I have a formula now to kill people and dissolve their dead bodies. My experiment is hundred percent successful. I am ready to take my revenge. They were all surprised to see me talk like that.

July 26th. I told my brother Haji Ejaz that I sleep on dead bodies every night. I have gone too far and he should be mentally prepared about any bad news about me any day. Then I talked to Zia. He listened to my story and was supportive. He said this world needs to end.

July 30th. Today my old employee Sarfaraz came. That bastard had deserted us a year and a half ago. I had met him in the holy shrine of Data Darbar. Those were the days I used to go there to donate food daily. He had joined me on my trips to Murree and Rahim Yar Khan. After we came back from the trips he ran away. I was quite

Dr. K. Sohail

upset by his disappearance. While Sarfaraz was sleeping Sabir put a chain around his neck and strangled him. I liked this method. It seemed quicker and more efficient than the poisonous gas. I told Sabir and Zafar to use this method now. Sarfarz and Shehzad were my old employees. I am glad to kill them because in spite of my favours they always tried to harm me. I feel more delighted in killing Pathans as I was killed by one of them.

August 1st.   Zafar brought a 19 years old boy from Shuja-abad. His name was Noman. Zafar and Sabir finished him off. It was Sunday. At 10 a.m., someone knocked on the door. It was Nasim Murshad. We showed him the dead body and shared the whole story. He patted me on my back and gave Sabir and Zafar two hundred rupees each. I was really happy to see that.

August 3rd.   Today we found a thirteen-year-old boy from Jhang Road Pind Baowala. Zafar and Sabir finished him off. The count reached 18 today.

August 4th.   Zafar and Sabir have promised that to take revenge they would help in flowing rivers of blood. They brought a boy from Multan. His name was Babar and he was 15. These vagabonds sometimes do not tell their addresses right. If I ask too many questions they get suspicious. And then I think that finding the address is not the most important part of this revenge. I had hired two boys to help them but they tried to kill me. Now before I die I am taking many of them with me. God gave me a second life after I was in a coma for 22 days. I am in such a miserable state that I can hardly walk or eat or see. I have a broken jaw. The fractures of my skull keep me disoriented. Such suffering also killed my mother. I am very grateful to Zafar and Sabir who are helping me in my plan.

August 6th.   Nasim Murshad came early in the morning today. He went with Zafar and Sabir and brought a 14-year-old boy named Ghulam Mohyuddin, son of Abdul Majeed. He was from Lahore and lived in Islampura. He told us his phone number was 550141. Nasim liked the boy, as he was beautiful. He took his pants off and took him inside the room. After an hour he invited Zafar and Sabir inside, and gave 8 sleeping pills. He was still awake when they forcefully put a gas mask and made him inhale poisonous gas. He had fits before he died. Murshad did not feel sorry for him and after he died put him in the drum.

Murshad has helped me for the last twenty years. He is even helping me in the last stages of my life. I will be indebted to him even after my death.

August 9th.   On my mother's death I was so heartbroken that when I met Liaqat Ali, my cousin, I told him the whole story. He supported me in killing all these boys. He said he was really upset when he heard that I was killed by my employees. I gained a lot of emotional support by his talk. May God bless him. Amen.

August 10th.   Zafar and Sabir went to Yadgar at 6 a.m. They brought a 16-year-old boy who belonged to Mardan. He was very healthy and looked like my murderer. We gave him sleeping pills in his food but they did not affect him. When he did not fall asleep, Zafar put a dog chain around his neck and strangled him. Then they went out again and brought another Pathan from Pindi. He was 14. He was strangled by a chain too and put in the drum with acid. Zafar and Sabir performed so well today that I gave them 500 rupees each as a reward.

August 11th.   Zafar did not come today. Sabir was working alone. He found thirteen-year-old Qasim on the street and brought him home. He gave him the sleeping pills and killed him with poisonous gas. With great difficulty we put his dead body in the drum.

August 12th.   Today there was a recitation of Holy Quran in the memory of Mom at Saeed's house. I went to the cere-

mony, read Quran and stayed from 4 p.m. to 8 p.m.
Today Ashiq and Maulvi Riaz came to see me from
Fatehgarh. Riaz thanked me for getting rid of the dead
body of the old man. Sabir wants to kill a few more
people. I gave them permission. Inshaallah [with the
grace of God] they will bring more dead bodies but
those bodies will not be part of my project.

August 13th.   Today Zafar brought a 12-year-old boy and gave him
films to watch. Other employees were sleeping in the
other room. In the middle of the night Zafar and I finished him off and put him in the drum. Then we poured
acid on him and went back to sleep. In the morning we
told other employees that the boy had left quite early.

Later on we sent the employees out and Sabir and
Zafar brought another 20-year-old boy. His name was
Abdul Jabbar and he was from Faisalabad. He was
given sleeping pills and finished with poisonous gas.
Later during the day, Sabir met two more boys, 18-
year-old Ramazan and 14-year-old Tauqeer. We offered
them milkshakes with eight sleeping pills and when
they fell asleep, we chained them and them gave them
poisonous gas with the mask. After they died Sabir and
I put them in the drums with great difficulty.

August 17th.   On 13th of August we had killed four boys and it took
us four days to dissolve their bodies. The acid turned
black. We had to throw it in the gutter and pour in
more acid. But it boosted our confidence. Today Sabir
brought two more boys. A thirteen-year-old, Sajjad,
and twelve-year-old Afzaal. We got rid of them and put
them in the drum.

August 18th.   Nasim Murshad came today and brought a 16-year-old
boy, Mansoor, with him. He was from Shakargarh.
Sabir, Nasim and I got rid of him and put him in the
drum. Later on we were by ourselves and spent time
throwing dark acid into the gutter and putting new
acid in the drums.

The Myth of the Chosen One   141

August 19th.	There was another religious ceremony in the memory of Mom. I went from 4 p.m. to 8 p.m. to recite Quran. Last night Sabir brought another two boys, 17-year-old Ramazan and 12-year-old Kashif. Sabir told them that his younger brother is missing and he would give them 100 rupees a day if they helped look for the brother. In the middle of the night when we went into their room, we found the older brother having sex with the younger one. We were shocked and slapped the older one. The younger brother told us that his brother takes him to places and then sexually abuses him. We were happy getting rid of them. Our count has reached 32. Later on we found Kamran Niazi, a beautiful boy from Faisal Abad. At 3:30 a.m. we strangled him. He was beautiful but our hearts have turned into stones. It was our 33rd murder.
August 23rd .	Today we found a beautiful fair coloured boy. His name was Ali Shair and he was 13. We met him in Yadgar where I had met my murderer. He was from Deepalpur. He went to sleep but at 3 a.m. when Zafar came we strangled him with the chain. He died within a minute. Now we use the chain more to do our job.
August 24th.	When my mom died I was so upset and hurt, I had planned to commit suicide. In front of my relatives I mentioned that I am capable of killing people and making dead bodies disappear. They all got worried. Later on I changed my mind about suicide but I am worried my relatives might hurt me with the information I gave them.
August 25th.	Zafar brought a 15-year-old boy. His name was Dilshad and he was from Sargodha. He came to get involved in sodomy. In the morning when Zafar came we got rid of him at 5 a.m. Zafar got rid of him. I get bugged by such boys. It was necessary to finish him off.
August 26th.	Today there was ceremony in the memory of Mom. I read Quran and asked forgiveness from God.

D r .   K .   S o h a i l

I am happy that I am taking revenge of my mom's death from these bastards who run away from home. Those bastards neither serve their parents nor anybody else. Today we got rid of three boys. The first one was Naseer Ahmed who was 15, the second was Zaheer Abbas from Shahdara Lahore and the third one was Haider Ali, 13, from Badami Bagh Lahore. Today our count reached 38.

[The entries for the following dates read much the same.] August 26th, August 29th,, August 30th, August 31st, September 2nd, September 7th, September 9th, September 12th,, September 13th, September 15th, September 18th, September 22nd, September 24th, September 25th, September 26th,September 27th, September 29th, September 30th, October 1st, October 3rd October 5th, October 6th, October 7th, October 9th, October 12th, October 16thOctober 17th, October 21st, October 23rd, October 24th, October 28th, October 29th, October 30th, November 1st, November 3rd, and November 5th.]

November 6th. Today all three of my nephews (Waseem Pervaiz, Shabbaz Aijaz, and Nomi Jabbar) came at 5 p.m. They brought a beautiful 16-year-old girl with them. The girl was very upset. Waseem took me aside and told me, "Uncle! We are in big trouble! Please help us!" When I asked the details, he said, "This girl is a friend of a girl who works in our house as a servant. She ran away from her village. She stayed at our place for awhile. I seduced her. Then I introduced her to Nomi and Shabbaz. We all slept with her. Then she left. Now she came back after three months and told us that she is pregnant. She wants us to do something, otherwise her parents will take us to court. She is asking me to marry her. We brought her here so that you can help. We know that you are helping people in getting rid of their enemies. Please get rid of this girl." Sajid told me that

Shahzad overheard our conversation and told him that we were going to get rid of that girl. I asked Waseem to take the chain and put it around the girl's neck from the back while I kept her busy talking. We closed the door. When Waseem acted on my suggestion, the girl struggled but Shabbaz, Nomi and I held onto her. We turned the TV up loud and choked her.

I told the boys that I also wanted to get rid of Shahzad. Waseem put the chain around his neck too, and we all helped him in killing Shahzad. Waseem put the chain around his neck too and we all helped him to kill Shahzad. Then we put both dead bodies in the drums and asked my three nephews to pour in the acid.

Because of them I could not take pictures of the girl and Shahzad, neither did I ask the girl for her address.

All three boys were very happy they succeeded in the project. I told them to keep it a secret. They promised they would not tell anyone and left.

November 13th. Today was Sunday. Nasim Murshad came at 9 a.m. Ehsan and Khaliq came at 11 a.m. We decided to kill a Pathan today. Ehsan and Murshad went and came back with a beautiful Pathan boy from Peshawar. His name was Yasir and he was 16. His father Safiullah Khan was a security officer. He was smart and beautiful. I took him to the other room and took his picture, then sent him to the other room where Khaliq, Ehsan and then Murshad sexually abused him. At 2 p.m. they put a black mask on his face and Khaliq and Ehsan strangled him. Then they put his dead body in the drum. We were happy that the count of one hundred was complete. We congratulated each other. I was so thankful to God for helping me complete my project that I had tears in my eyes. We celebrated all day long and ate sweets. In the evening everybody went home.

⏳ 23 "He is a Satan ..."
Excerpts from the Judge's verdict
Lahore, March 16, 2000

The following are excerpts from the text of the judgement given by Allah Bakhash Ranjha, the Additional Sessions Judge in the child-killing case:

"The *challan* [charge]of this case was sent up by Mr. Muhammad Aslam Awais Hussain, District Attorney, Lahore in the court of Mian Ghulam Hussain, Area Magistrate, Lahore. The learned Area Magistrate further sent up the same to the learned Sessions Judge Lahore, Mian Muhammad Jahangir under Section 190 (3) of Pakistan Penal Code".

"Mian Muhammad Jahangir, learned Sessions Judge Lahore entrusted this case to this court on 8-2-2000, in order to conduct the trial in accordance with the law. The accused were produced before this court on 9-2-2000. Copies of the statements of the prosecution witnesses recorded by the Investigating officer under Section 161 Pakistan Penal Code and other relevant documents were delivered to the accused persons provided under Section 265-C Pakistan Penal Code on 9-2-2000. It was inquired from the accused that whether they were in a position to engage their counsel or not. The accused persons stated that they were not in a position to engage their counsel in order to defend the case on their behalf.

Hence, the court appointed the following Advocates on State expenses to defend the case on their behalf:

Mr. Najeeb Faisal Chaudhry Advocate for accused Javed Iqbal Mughal (the principal accused).

Mr. Abdul Baqi Advocate for accused Shehzad alias Guddu alias Sajid.

Mr. Asghar Ali Gill Advocate for accused Muhammad Nadeem alias Deem, and

Mr. Safdar Javed Chaudhry Advocate for accused Muhammad Sabir."

"Keeping in view the sensitivity of the case and the number of prosecution witnesses besides Mr. Muhammad Ashraf Tahir, Assistant: Public Prosecutor [APP], Mr.Burhan Moazzam Malik, Mr. Muhammad Asghar Rokeri, Mr. Amjad Chatta, Maj (Rtd) Aftab Ahmed and Mr. M. Iqbal Cheema Advocates were appointed as Special Public Prosecutors [SPP] and in this respect a letter was written to the Registrar, Lahore High Court, Lahore through the learned Sessions Judge Lahore in order to inform the Government to make the appropriate proceedings in this regard."

"The charge against the accused persons was framed on 17-2-2000 to which they did not plead guilty and claimed to be tried, therefore, the prosecution evidence was recorded. A calendar of 122 prosecution witnesses was appended along with the challan, out of which, 105 prosecution witnesses were produced by the prosecution in the court while 17 prosecution witnesses were given up being unnecessary. The prosecution also tendered certain documents in evidence which will be discussed in detail in this judgement."

"Muhammad Ashiq Marth Inspector was posted as Station House Officer [SHO] at Police Station [PS], Ravi Road, Lahore, on 2-12-1999. On receiving the information that house No. 16-B Ravi Road, Lahore, which was in possession of accused Javed Iqbal, was locked for the last so many days and acute smell was coming from the said house. He along with police party consisting of Taj Din, Sub-Inspector, [DSI] and Muhammad Siddique, Assistant Sub-Inspector, [ASI] etc. reached at the spot. The outer door of the house was unlocked and he entered in the house along with his companions. He observed there that in certain rooms of the house, posters were fixed on the walls allegedly written by Javed Iqbal Mughal accused, with regard to the murder of human beings, in respect of [one] hundred boys. On further checking he found two drums lying in the last room of the house, having liquid of acid, wherein, parts of dead bodies of the human being were present, as mentioned in the above said posters. In this view of the matter, he prepared a complaint Ex.P-A [Exhibits P-A] and sent the same to the Police Station through Muhammad Afzal ASI for the registration of the case.

He started the investigation. He prepared the inquest report regarding the big drum Ex. P-UUUU, attested by Mir Jehan and Abdul Jabbar PWs [Prosecution Witnesses]. He took into possession Kara [iron ring] P-161, having a black stone P-162 present in the leg of dead body lying in the drum. It was taken into possession vide [legal term used to direct reader's attention] recovery memo Ex. P-ZZZ, attested by PWs [Prosecution Witnesses]. Then he prepared the other inquest report Ex.P-VVVVV regarding small drum, attested by the PWs. After conducting the necessary proceedings and preparing the above said documents, he handed over both the drums along with the parts of the dead bodies to Shaukat Ali ASI and Zia Ullah Constable in order to escort the same to the dead house through application Ex. P-WWWWW and Ex.P-YYYYY. Drawings and marginal notes over the site plan are in his handwriting. It is also signed by him. He had taken into possession the drums which were containing the parts of dead bodies [identified by] vide recovery memo Ex.P-AAAA and Ex.P-BBBB, attested by the PWs. The drums are P-159 and P-160. He also took into possession 14 cans P-163/1-14, allegedly containing liquid regarding which accused Javed Iqbal had stated in his diaries that these contained human blood and fragments. He sealed the case property with stamp "NH". He also secured earth mixed with Chemical P-165 from the site and made into a sealed parcel and took into possession vide recovery memo Ex. P-CCCC, attested by the PWs. Two pieces of rubber pipe P-166 and P-167, three scissors P-168/1-3, one bunch of copper wire P-69 stained with earth, fluid and human hair, were detached and he took above said articles into possession vide recovery memo Ex.P-DDDD, attested by the PWs. He also took into possession one bottle containing liquid P-170, frying pan P-171, one big tyre P-173, two jugs stained with human hair P-174/1-2, one mask stained with human hair P-175, one Tube Samad Bond P-172, one iron rod [weighing] more than 5 KG [kilograms] P-176, two iron weights, two KG each P-177/1-2, one strainer stained with human hair P-178, one keef [ladle] stained with human hair P-179, plastic pipe P-180, two under-wears P-181/1-2, two pants P-182/1-2, one shirt P-183, one doal [bucket] P-184, one bucket P-185, one iron rod P-186, one rod with a curved hook P-187, one wooden dunda [stick] P-188, one packet noodles P-189, one wiper stained with human hair, vide recovery memo Ex.P-EEEE, attested by PWs. Human hair were separated from the said articles, sealed into parcel with stamp "NH" and were taken into possession vide recovery memo P-FFFF by the witness."

"From the second room he took into possession eight posters affixed on the walls, which were of white colour written with black marker which are P-191/1-8 and other four posters of pink colour written with black marker, affixed on the walls, which are P-192/1-4. On these posters Javed Iqbal accused allegedly narrated about the murder of human beings. He took the same into possession vide recovery memo Ex.P-GGGG, attested by the PWs."

"He also took into possession from the second room, three plastic bags P-191/1-3 which contained one hundred pair of clothes of the alleged murdered children which are P-194/1-100. He also took into possession two plastic bags P-195/1-2, which contained 77 pairs of footwears P-196/1-54, one shoe polish box P-197, one iron cantor P-198, two empty bottles P-199/1-2, vide recovery memo Ex.P-HHHH, attested by the PWs."

"He also took into possession from the first room of the house from a bed of wooden, one chain sixteen inches in length P-200, regarding which allegedly the accused disclosed in his diary that the same was weapon of offence, through the recovery memo Ex.P-JJJJ, after converting the same into a sealed parcel with the stamp of "NH". From the said room he also took into possession from the drawer of the bed, one album containing 57 photographs P-201/1-57, three diaries allegedly written by Javed Iqbal accused P-202/1-3. In one diary there were names and addresses of one hundred children, in a second diary the accused narrated about committing of murder of all the children. There was also writing on the back side of these photographs mentioned above. All the above said articles were taken into possession vide recovery memo Ex.P-KKKK by the investigating officer. He also took into possession from the said room of the house of Javed Iqbal accused from underneath the bed, seven x-ray films related to Javed Iqbal accused P-203/1-7 through recovery memo Ex.P-LLLL, attested by

Dr. K. Sohail

the PWs. He further took into possession two empty packets of Valium-10, P-206/1-2, vide recovery memo Ex.P-MMMM, attested by the PWs."

"During the inspection of the house from the roof of the house of Javed Iqbal, the investigating officer took into possession some stone like articles and out of the same three P-207/1-3 were sealed into a parcel with the stamp of mark " NH", vide recovery memo Ex.P-NNNN, attested by the PWs. He also took into possession from the house sixty-five household articles P-208/1-65, vide recovery memo Ex.P-OOOO attested by PWs.10. On 3-12-99, two dockets Ex.P-ZZZZZ /1-2 were issued from the office of SP City, Lahore for the getting the post mortem of the fragments/ remains of human being found lying in the drums recovered from the house of accused Javed Iqbal. They were forwarded by the investigating officer PW/105 and were sent to the doctor concerned. On the same day he brought the draftsman Hameed ud din Chishti at the place of occurrence who took the rough notes of the place of occurrence for preparing the site plan [floor plan of Javed Iqbal's home]."

"On the same day some parents and relatives of the deceased children visited police station Ravi Road, Lahore and identified various articles belonging to the deceased children which were allegedly taken into possession by PW-104 from the place of Javed Iqbal accused. He prepared the identification memos in this respect, the detail of which is as under:"

"Abdul Aziz identified the photo P-72 of his son Abdul Majeed vide memo Ex.P/LL, Zaheer Hussain PW identified shalwar P-35, kurta P-34 of his son Rameez vide memo Ex.PU, Rashid Ilias Sheea identified one picture P-52 of his son Dilawar vide memo Ex.PAA, Mohammad Yaqub PW identified the photograph P-57 of his son Mohammad Azhar vide memo Ex.PEE, Ghulam PW identified shalwar P-59 shirt P-60 and photographs P-61 of his son Imran Ilias Jhara vide memo Ex.PGG, Mohammad Amin PW identified shalwar

P-65, shirt P-66, chappal [sandal] P-67/1-2 and photograph P-68 of his nephew Mohammad Ahmed vide memo Ex.P-JJ. Nazir Ahmed PW identified shalwar P-69, shirt P-70, photograph P-71 of his nephew

Tanweer vide memo Ex.P-KK, Amir Hamza PW identified photo P-74 of his son Shakil Hassa vide memo Ex.P-NN."

"Masood Aziz PW-105 was posted as DSP [District Superintendent of Police], CIA, Model Town, Lahore on 9-12-99 when he received an order from SSP Lahore to conduct further investigation of his case. He conducted the investigation of this case during the period of 9-12-99 to 27-12-99 at different times and tried to arrest the accused persons. On 28-12-99, through a telephonic message he directed Mohammad Ashraf Zahid Inspector/ SHO, PS Ravi Road to again visit the place of occurrence, resident of the accused Javed Iqbal i.e., 16-B Ravi Road, Lahore in order to collect any further proof regarding this case."

"On 30-12-99, he received an information from Sohava from the local police of Sohava Police Station that Sajid and Nadeem accused present in the court, were apprehended there from a bank while they were trying to encash a traveller's cheque (the accused Sajid and Nadeem were duly identified by the witness before the court). At this SSP Lahore formed a team for the arrest of the above said accused for taking them to Lahore from Sohava. On the same day at about 8.45/9 p.m., they received an information that Javed Iqbal accused, (present in the court, to whom the witness identified before the court), had appeared in the office of newspaper namely Daily Jang, Lahore. He along with a police party and Mohammad Zaheer Sub Inspector reached at the office of Daily Jang, Lahore. Some army officers were present there outside the premises of the office of Daily Jang, Lahore, who informed them that Javed Iqbal accused was making his statement before the journalists and he should wait outside, till the completion of his statement. The administration of Daily Jang handed over accused Javed Iqbal to them. They took the accused to the headquarters of CIA, Cantt. After reaching at CIA office, he made the personal search of the accused and during the search he recovered from the front pocket of the shirt of the accused, one photostat of debit voucher of the name of Javed Iqbal P-6, one photostat of a travellers cheque of Rs [Rupees] 10,000 P-7 cash of Rupees 148 in Pakistani currency P-8/1-20, one pury [packet]of powder like poison which was recovered from the side pocket of shirt of accused P-9, one plastic small box containing 80 intoxicant tablets P-10 1-80, one eye band with an elastic P-11, one key ring along 3 pieces of keys P-12 1-4, and one wrist watch from the left hand of the accused P-13. He prepared the recovery memo of his personal search and also converted P-10, P-9 into parcels and sealed the same. The recovery memo was attested by Zaheer Ahmed Sub-Inspector and Shaukat Ali Constable. He further stated that the personal search of the accused was made at the office of CIA and not at the office of Daily Jang keeping in view the safety of the accused. In the meanwhile, Sajid and Nadeem accused were also handed over to him by the raiding party headed by Syed Jamat Ali Shah DSP [District Superintendent of Police] CIA Cantt. He formally arrested Javed Iqbal accused, Nadeem accused and Sajid accused and recorded their statements."

"On 31-12-99, he obtained the physical remand of the above said 3 accused persons from the area magistrate. He also made an application for getting the above said 3 accused persons medically examined which was allowed and on the same day all the 3 accused were medically examined by Surgeon Medicolegal Punjab, Lahore. He obtained the MLR [Medical Legal Report] of Javed Iqbal accused which is Ex.PG and Ex.PH and the application are Ex.PG/1 and Ex.PH/1 respectively and MLR of Shahzad accused are Ex.P-I and Ex.P-J and applications in this respect are Ex.P-I/1 and Ex. P-J/1. All the applications are signed by PW."

"On the same day, Jamil Chishti PW, Editor Crimes, Daily Jang, Lahore and Asad Sahi, Crime Report Daily Jang, PW given up, appeared before him and produced a copy of Daily Jang, Lahore dated 31.12.1999 which was taken by him into possession vide recovery memo Ex.P-00000 and the copy of newspaper is P-226, attested by the witnesses. PW-105 also recorded their statements under Section 161 Pakistan Penal Code He handed over the above said clothes of Javed Iqbal and Shehzad accused to the Moharrar [stores-keeper] for keeping in safe custody and for onward transmission to the concerned office."

"On 11.1.2000, on the disclosure of accused Javed during interrogation, he went along with the accused and Akthar PW to the house of sister of the accused namely Mst. Yasmin Alias Nanhi situated at Sher Shah Road, Shad Bagh, Lahore. The accused led them to the upper story of the house in a room, where, an iron box was lying. It was locked. It was opened through a key by the accused, which was provided to the accused by a briefcase P-1137. The briefcase was opened and from this briefcase, he recovered a Sangli [chain] P-138, Mask P-140, Camera P-142, one pistol 22 bore P-139, powder like poison P-141, advertisement for search of Sarfraz Ahmed P-146/1-25, one envelope Kinkia P-144, five sets of negatives P-147/1-22, 234/125, 235/1-31, 144/1-31, 337/1-23 and 138, one memorandum containing 35 pages P-150/1-35, 10 markers P-151/1-10, one visiting card P-148, three audio cassettes P-155/1-3, one Press Card P-149, licence of pistol P-145, two photo copies of National Identity Card of accused Javed Iqbal P-146/1-2, one photo copy of traveller's cheque P-147, two rings P-147, two rings P-147/1-2, one adhesive tape P-148, one scissors P-152, one book P-153, which were taken into possession by the Investigating Officer/PW-155. He converted Sangli, Mask, powder like poison and pistol into sealed parcel. The recorded articles were taken into possession vide recovery memo Ex.PYY, attested by the PWs. He also prepared the site plan without scale of the place of recovery, which is Ex.P-YYY/1. He handed over the case property to the Moharrar for keeping it in the safe custody in the Mal-Khana [storage] and for onward transmission to the concerned officers, after returning to his office CIA, Cantt, Lahore."

"On 12.1.2000, Muhammad Sabir accused was produced by his father at CIA Office Model Town, Lahore. The Investigating Officer formally arrested him, interrogated him and recorded his first version. Therefore he got his physical remand. On the same day, he also interrogated accused Javed Iqbal. The accused disclosed in the presence of PWs that in case of any difficulty to put the bodies in the drums, they used to cut the dead bodies into pieces by Toka [cleaver] which he had thrown in Ravi River. On this disclosure, he brought the accused at old bridge of Ravi River as pointed out by the accused. A diver namely Allah Ditta PW was arranged but in spite of the best efforts, Toka could not be recovered. A "Farad Nishan Dehi" [Plan of Investigation] and rough site plan were prepared in this respect.

"On 13.1.2000, all the four accused were produced before the area magistrate in the early hours and in the afternoon their confessional statements were recorded by the area magistrate."

"The witness further stated that all the accused turn by turn pointed out the places where they used to strangulate, etc., boys in order to commit their murder and then used to cut the bodies into pieces and then to put them into the drum. Two rooms of the house of Javed Iqbal accused were pointed out by the accused persons turn by turn. He also prepared a rough site plan in this respect. The accused persons, except Sabir, also pointed out a drain near Yadgar where they used to dispose the fluid of the dead bodies. He prepared the pointation memo and rough site plan of those places. Then he came back along with the accused persons at CIA office Cantt: where the accused stated before the witness that their conscious was pricking them and they want to make confessional statements before the magistrate. He produced them before the area magistrate. The area magistrate granted the judicial remand of the accused on the application of the witness, which is Ex.-PGGGGG. The witness and other police officials present along with him were asked to leave the court room and the area magistrate recorded the statements of the accused persons under Section 164 Pakistan Penal Code and after recording the statement, on the request of the witness, the area magistrate handed over the attested copies of the statements of the accused persons to him. Therefore the accused were sent to judicial lock up."

"On 14.1.2000, Jamil Chishti PW was associated in the Investigation of this case and he handed over to the Investigating Officer PW-105 audio cassette P-227 and Video Cassette P-228, which he took into possession vide recovered memos Ex.P-QQQQQ. He recorded the statement of Jamil Chishti under Section 161 Pakistan Penal Code at the relevant times and handed over the case property to the Moharrar at the relevant times for keeping the same in safe custody and for onward transmission to the concerned office. He also received the reports from the concerned offices and handed over the entire record of this case to Station House Officer, Police Station Ravi road,

Lahore in order to prepare the report under Section 173 Pakistan Penal Code for onward submission in the court for judicial verdict. The same was prepared by Muhammad Ashraf Zahid PW Inspector/SHO, PS Ravi Road, Lahore. The witness being the Senior Officer Muhammad Ashraf Zahid identified his handwriting and signatures over the challan. The witness lastly stated that before the submission of the challan, after obtaining the legal opinion from DSP, Legal, he deleted Section 7 of Anti Terrorist Activities, Act, 1997 and added Section 364-A and Section 12, Offence of Zina [rape] (Enforcement of Hadud [Islamic Law]), Ordinance VII of 1979 and Section 388 of Pakistan Penal Code and sent the case to the competent authorities for further proceedings."

"The witness further stated that he does not remember the exact words of the interview in the verbatim, however, the accused stated before him that some SHO of PS Ghazi Abad, Lahore had misbehaved the accused with regard to an incident in which one servant of the accused was injured the accused and on the complaint of the accused no justice was done to the accused. The accused operated upon due to said injury but he could not rehabilitate completely. His mother died due to this shock. Even then the police did not listen to him and his grievance was not redressed. It came to his mind to take the revenge of death of his mother because the death of his mother had given him great shock. In order to take the revenge, he arranged a house at Ravi Road, Lahore, where he committed the murder of one hundred children. The accused stated this before the witness without any duress or pressure or any sort of influence. The accused again stated that in fact his mother died due to that shock and he would make one hundred mothers weep and wail. When it was asked from the accused that how he had committed this act, the accused answered and informed the names of his co-accused, i.e., Sajid, Sabir and Nadeem. Then the accused narrated the method of committing this offence. The accused stated that he used to put gas mask on their faces and when they used to become unconscious, they were strangulated. Then the dead bodies were put in the drums containing chemicals and the same used to dissolve and then they (the accused persons) used to destroy the dead bodies. The accused further stated before the witness that initially he

Dr. K. Sohail

was not having the camera but after 43, he obtained the photographs of the children who were later on murdered. The accused further stated before the witness that he murdered one hundred children. On the inquiry of the witness that why accused had not committed further murders, the accused replied that still he had sufficient amount to purchase the acid for further murders but as the accused had fixed the target to commit the murder of one hundred children at the time of death of his mother and for that reason he completed this target."

"The witness further stated that due to some apprehensions, they made the personal search of the accused and found so many intoxicant tablets which were in the socks of the accused. The accused further stated before him that he (accused) having the intention to put a heavy weight around his neck and to commit the suicide in Ravi River but he could not do so. The accused further informed that his jaw was broken and he does not feel himself to be an alive person. The accused used the word 'when he was murdered' in his interview."

"Syed Khalil Shehzad PW-90 also runs a photographic shop by the name and style of Supreme Colour Lab at 314-Ravi Road, Lahore. (Before starting his statement, the witness requested the Court to record his statement by placing his hand on Holy Quran) and he started his statement while placing his hand on Holy Quran. He stated that he worked at the above said shop of developing and printing of Camera Films. Accused Javed Iqbal (identified by the witness by placing hand on the shoulder of the accused) came to him and asked to make the prints of all the negatives. In fact the customers normally asked them to make the prints of the good negatives while the accused asked him to prepare all the prints of the photographs. The accused got his name recorded on the envelope as Javed Iqbal. That envelope was later on taken into custody by the police during the investigation. It was probably 22nd or 23rd November, 1999 and he is sure that he prepared 31 prints. All the negatives which were developed by him are P-209/1-31 and all the positives/photographs which were developed/printed by him are P-27, P-61, P-68, P-72, P-77, P-80, P-84, P-90, p-93, P-98, P-100, P-107, P-111, P-114, P-116/A, P-199, P-128, P-136, P-53, P-56, P-57, P-

210, P-211, P-212, P-213, P-214, P-215, P-216, P-217 andP-216, identified by the witness in the court. His statement was recorded by the police in this respect."

"PW-83 Mirza Nazir Baig is employee at Pasha Chemical, owned by one Muhammad Naeem, situated at Circular Road, Lahore near Adds Crown Bus. He stated that the owner of the shop Muhammad Naeem used to deal with the work of factories and in the absence of owner he along with another employee used to sell the different kinds of chemical at the shop. He further stated that accused Sajid used to purchase sulphuric acid and hydrochloric acid from his shop. They have got a license to sell the acid and his statement was recorded by the police. (The witness identified the accused Sajid by putting his hand on the should of the accused)."

"Mulammad Rafiq SI was posted at office of CIA, Model Town, Lahore on 12.1.2000. Accused Javed Iqbal was being interrogated in his presence by Masood Aziz PSP. In his presence accused Javed Iqbal disclosed that he had thrown the Bugda [cleaver] in River Ravi with which he used to cut the dead bodies into pieces and he could point out the said place. The witness, the accused and the IO [Interrogating Officer] along with other police party reached Ravi River. The witness summoned Allah Ditta Diver PW who tried to search the Budga in the river but Bugda could not be found. His statement was recorded by the I.O".

"After closing the prosecution case, statements of the accused persons under section 342 Pakistan Penal Code were recorded".

"All the accused stated that they are innocent". The accused Javed Iqbal admitted that charts/posters, household articles, clothes and shoes of the children were present in his house and police recovered the same from his house. He further stated that photographs were not recovered from his house but he himself posted the same to DIG, Lahore and to the newspaper, the Daily Jang and DIG, Lahore and SP. CIA, Lahore. He admitted all the recoveries except human fragments/ remains, human hair, mask, and iron chain. He also admitted that there was some acid in his house in one can. He further stated that his confessional statement before the Area Magistrate was not volunteer statement but he was pressurized by the police to get record of this statement and it was threatened by the police that he would be killed in fake police encounter in case he did not record this statement. He also stated that his extra judicial statement/interview in office of Daily Jang, Lahore was also not recorded in its true perspective. He denied the murder of any boy or ever they came to him. In addition of his verbal statement before the court, he tendered his written statement consisting of 20 pages, which is part of his statement as provided under Section 342 Pakistan Penal Code He did not appear as liaison witness as provided under Section 340 (2) Pakistan Penal Code nor produced any evidence in defense. He admitted that he himself appeared in the office of Daily Jang, Lahore 30.12.1999, from where, he was arrested by the police.

"Accused Shehzad alias Sajid Alias Guddu denied all the allegations against him levelled by the prosecution during the evidence. He denied all the recoveries stating being incorrect and being not in his knowledge. He further stated that he does not know about three diaries. He went to bring one diary on the instance of Javed Iqbal co-accused had written letters to the police. He further stated that he was falsely implicated in this case only for the reason that he had gone for the encashment of a traveller's cheque of the accused Javed Iqbal.

"Accused Nadeem also denied the allegations levelled against him by the prosecution during the evidence and stated that he has only been involved in this case as they went to UBL Branch, Sohawa, District Jhelum in order to encash a traveller's cheque of his co-accused Javed Iqbal and was arrested there.

"Accused Sabir also denied the allegation levelled against him by the prosecution and further stated he was arrested by the police and informed him that Javed Iqbal accused had disclosed his name and involved him in the case. On inquiry by the police he only stated that Faisal is his friend.

"As during the statement Jamil Chisthi PW-97 it came into evidence that besides P-228, another video film was also prepared by Jang authorities and it was admitted by the PW that the same is available in the office of newspaper, hence Ajmal Taufeeq Admnistration Officer Jang was called and examined as CW-1 who produced video cassette CW-1/A.

I have heard the arguments advanced by learned APP [Assistant Public Prosecutor] and learned SPPs [Special Public Prosecutor] on behalf of the state and learned defense counsel for each accused at considerable length and have gone through the whole record.

The case was opened by Mian Muhammad Ashraf Tahir, learned PP [Public Prosecutor] for the State and argued that the prosecution in order to provide the charge against the accused persons produced as many as 105 witnesses and the remaining 17 witnesses were given up as being unnecessary. He further argued that the accused present in the court committed the most heinous offence of the present era and 100 innocent minor children were done to death with no fault of them hence the accused deserve no leniency and that they should be punished severely in accordance with law. The learned APP further submitted that prosecution with the help of evidence produced before the court has fully established its case beyond any shadow of doubt and has fully succeeded in bringing home the guilt of the accused. He further argued that prosecution in the instant case has produced strong and confidence inspiring evidence in the shape of judicial confession, extra judicial recoveries and other circumstantial evidence and the witnesses stood the test of lengthy cross examination by the learned counsel for the defense but they failed to cause any dent in the edifice of the prosecution case. He further argued that the admission of accused Javed Iqbal at the time of framing of charge and at the time of statement under Section 342 Pakistan Penal Code corroborates the version of the prosecution. In the instant case the witnesses are independent having no malice against the accused and their testimony cannot be doubted and their evidence cannot be brushed aside. He further requested the court that capital punishment be awarded to the accused."

"Mr. Burhan Moazzam Malik, Special Public Prosecutor, while arguing on the point of motive and modus operandi invited the attention of this court to the factors which prompted and forced Javed Iqbal to commit his gruesome and loathsome murder of 100 innocent children without any rhyme or reason. It happened in 1997 when the accused Javed Iqbal was given physical beating by his two employees and one of the employee Arbab was also given physical beating. Javed Iqbal was badly injured and consequently he was admitted in the hospital where he was not cordially dealt with and he was not completely rehabilitated as a result of apathetic behaviour of the police as well as the doctors, his mother was seriously shocked and consequently she bewailed and expired later on. Javed Iqbal accused, took the incident of death of his mother seriously and vowed and determined that he would make the mothers of hundred children bewail like his mother had bewailed and in order to take his revenge and to achieve his evil ends he formed a plan in his mind by inducing, kidnapping the minor boys belonging to different cities, who left their houses for one reason or the other from the shrine of Data Darbar, Railways Station, Shahdara Station, Minar-e-Pakistan and Fruit Mandi, bringing them to his house at 16-B Ravi Road, Lahore committing sodomy with them, taking their photographs, administering intoxicants in the tea and in the cold water, putting the gas mask on the mouths of the boys and making them unconscious and lastly causing their death by strangulation and by fire arms in order to destroy the evidence by putting the dead bodies in the chemical/acid, which dissolved the bodies and throwing dissolved liquid through gutters".

The following are excerpts from the rebuttal by the defense.

"...The prosecution has also failed to produce the hundred parents of a hundred missing children in order to prove that still a number of missing children is one hundred. Therefore the possibility that so many of them had gone back to their houses, cannot be ruled out.

"Learned defense counsel for Javed Iqbal accused Mr. Najeeb Faisal Chaudhry further argued that the prosecution has failed to produce further any corroborative evidence. There is no direct evidence in this case and even it cannot be said that the dead bodies were recovered from the house of accused lying in the drums. According to the report of chemical examiner and statement of doctor PW-16 the human hair were not traceable in the material sent to the chemical examiner. It is further admitted by the doctor that human hair are the part of the human body which dissolve at the last. The human hair in the said material was not traceable.

"The learned defense counsel next argued that the prosecution has produced a video P-228 recorded by Fahim Ahmad Sheikh PW-102 and got prepared by Jamil Ahmad Chishti, Crime Editor Daily Jang PW-99. The entire videocassette in the shape of interview got recorded by Jamil Ahmad Chishti had not been produced in the court. The court itself has observed that the accused were being controlled from his shoulder by Jamil Ahmad Chishti PW-99 during the interview. Therefore, it cannot be said that the said extra judicial confession was voluntarily without any coercion, inducement or pressure.

"The accused remained in police custody on physical remand for 14 days. During this period the accused was given threats and he was aware of the fate of another person Ishaq alias Billa and he was apprehensive that he will be murdered in police encounter and for that reason his statement under Section 164 Pakistan Penal Code was got recorded on the dictation of the police. In fact the police had given to the Magistrate the statement which the police wanted to be recorded U/S 164 Pakistan Penal Code The accused has further stated in his statement U/S 243 Pakistan Penal Code that he had only spoken ... before the Magistrate and he had not got recorded his entire statement as it has been produced before the court.

"It is an admitted fact that the present case is totally based on circumstantial evidence and there exists no direct evidence in this case. The learned defense counsel while arguing on this point categorically submitted that in the absence of any direct evidence no person can be convicted. It is next argued that no person can be convicted in the absence of any medical evidence; where there is no dead body available and no actual cause of death can be determined. No allegation regarding the killing of any human being can be levelled against any of the accused person. Learned defense counsel further argued that the prosecution has failed to produce any direct evidence in this case regarding the commission of any offence and circumstantial evidence on which the prosecution is trying to base their case is of no help to it.

"Though the courts are supposed to follow the well settled principle of jurisprudence, namely that an accused person is presumed to be innocent, that the prosecution is to provide a criminal case against an accused person beyond reasonable doubt and in case two views are possible, the view which favours the accused person would be preferred, and that all benefits of doubts should be extended to the accused, but, at the same time, the court should also taken notice of the changing circumstances of the present days. Even in cases where eyewitnesses are available they refuse to appear as witnesses in support of prosecution case, either because of fear or on account of being won over by the accused party. The court's approach, while appraising the evidence, should be dynamic and not static. It should keep in view all the facts and circumstances of the case and if it is satisfied that factually the person charged with the offence has committed the same, it should record the conviction though there might have been some technical lapses on the part of the investigation agency/prosecution, provided the same have not prejudiced the accused in fair trial. The people are losing faith in the criminal judicial system for the reason that in most of the cases the criminals get away without being punished on mere technicalities.

"The other Medical Officer appeared in this case is Dr. Imtiaz Bhatti, PW-11, who medically examined Javed Iqbal, Nadeem alias Deemi and Shehzad alias Sajid, accused on 31-12-1999 and found them potent. On the same day, he also examined Shahid alias Sajid and Nadeem alias Deemi, accused, and found that sodomy has been committed with both these accused persons. The prosecution also tendered in evidence the medical reports prepared by the Medical Officer and all the respective applications in this regard. The counsel for the accused did not counter the report of the above said Medical Officer but only suggested that he conducted the medical examination without the permission of the accused persons. So keeping in view the fact that PW11 has no animus [attitude] against any of the accused person and is a medical expert, I fully believe in his statement and find no force in the arguments advanced by learned counsel for accused.

"It was further argued on behalf of the accused persons that Dr. Moammad Riaz, PW-12, Assistant Professor Anatomy, King Edward Medical College, Lahore has opined that 'the pieces of the bones were difficult to identify as far as their age and sex were concerned and their human nature was also difficult to determine. Moreover, the stones like material provided does not contain bone as such.' Relying upon the above said opinion and on the second opinion that these small bones were not belonging to the human nature, it has been argued that the bones, which were recovered in this case have been found by the Medical Officer as not of human nature. So the case against the accused has become one of doubtful nature. But the learned SPP has submitted that after about 25 days of the lodging of FIR on 28-12-1999, Mohammad Zahid Ashraf, Inspector/SHO of Police Station Ravi Road visited again the place of occurrence for a second inspection and he found there these small bones in the drain of the kitchen, which he converted into sealed parcels and these bones were sent to the doctor PW-12, and these were not the bones, which were recovered from the drums, in which the human limbs were.

"I have heard both the parties. But I do not find myself in total agreement with the learned SPP on this point because there was no point in collecting the bones from the place of occurrence after about 25 days of the first inspection specially when the case of the prosecution is that on 02-12-1999 the Investigating Officer took almost every available material into possession from 16-B Ravi Road, Lahore and these 6 bones which are not found of human origin are in fact the over-doing of the police and I think this is a sheer plantation by the Police Officer because there was the Investigating Officer of this case and when the Investigating Officer was available in Lahore, what was the point in sending a Police Officer, who was not the Investigating Office by only a telephonic message to the place of occurrence, which as per the prosecution case, was sealed at that time. So here I do not believe this portion of prosecution story but I am afraid that this over-doing of the police is of no benefit to the defense because it was never the case of the prosecution that the bones sent to the doctor for determination were of human origin but they simply took some bones into possession, sent the same to the doctor without any particular cause. I also depreciate this practice of the police where by they tried to show extra efficiency.

"Now I take the evidence produced by the prosecution against Nadeem accused. In this connection the evidence of Taraiq Mahmood PW-33, Muhammad Fayyaz PW-98 and Tahir Ali PW-99 can be referred. PW-33 is a rickshaw driver by profession and he deposed that Nadeem accused met him near Yadgar and asked him to transport five chemical cans towards back side of Yadgar and took him to his house 16-B Ravi Road from where five cans were loaded in the rickshaw by the PW and were unloaded near Trash Drum of LMC near Ravi Chargha House. Prosecution also produced Muhammad Fayyaz PW-98 who deposed that Nadeem along with Javed Iqbal and Sahid accused took him and his brother Ijaz on the pretext that Javed Iqbal is suffering from paralysis and that he wants a massage on his body. The witness further stated that the accused took them to their house 16-B Ravi Road where he was sent back by the accused person saying that Ijaz will come later on but his brother did not turn up. The witness later on identified the iron ring P-233 with the stone, which was set in the aforesaid ring. The witness is a poor labourer. He was not previously known to Nadeem and other co-accused. He had no malice against the accused nor any enmity existed between them. It can, therefore, safely be held that the evidence of the witness is trustworthy and unimpeachable which find supports from the judicial confession of the accused Nadeem. And lastly the prosecution produced Tahir Ali PW-99 who deposed that Sajid and Nadeem accused used to purchase fruit from him and he had seen Yasir and Imran deceased in their accompany. The deposition of the witness is fully corroborated by the judicial confession of Nadeem accused. So I, therefore, hold that the evidence of the witness is unimpeachable and also inspire confidence and cannot be brushed aside. The prosecution also produced Mirza Nazir Baig PW-83, Muhammad Fayyaz PW-98 and Tahir Ali PW-99 against Sajid accused. Nazir Baig categorically deposed that Sajid accused used to purchase acid from him. His shop Pasha Chemical situated at Adda Crown Bus. Prosecution also produced Muhammad Fayyaz PW-98 who deposed that Sajid, Javed Iqbal and Nadeem had come to him and his brother Ijaz and took them to their house 16-B Ravi Road on the pretext that Javed Iqbal is suffering from paralysis and that he wants a massage and the accused took them to their house and he was sent back by the accused on the ground that Ijaz will come later on. The witness has later on identified the clothes and iron ring P-161 which the deceased used to wear on his leg. I am of the opinion that going on Fayyaz PW with the accused to their house is the over doing at the hand of police and the police had intentionally fabricated this evidence.

"In my humble opinion, I also noted the demeanor of all the heirs who appeared before me as witnesses. It was very difficult to control them as every one of them was willing to take the accused person in his own clutches and to convert them into pieces and the class of society to which all the deceased children belong is such who live their lives below the level of poverty and due to the excess of children and lack of resources most of them were even not in a position to approach the concerned police station for getting a FIR registered in this connection. Here I also want to express my opinion regarding the irresponsibility and indifferent attitude of police who miserably failed to search even a single boy who left his house on some pretext and rather they put such a cold shoulder and avoided their liabilities in such a manner that even legal heirs appearing before me complained of the fact that they approached the police for registration of FIR regarding the missing of their child but the police refused to do so. This is an alarming situation and I would write separately in this regarding to the concerned authorities.

"On the point of age of the accused person, learned defense counsel had argued that the age limit of three accused namely Shahzad,

Sabir and Nadeem is less than 18 years, therefore, they are minors and capital punishment cannot be awarded to them in the light of the provision contained in Section 306 PPC. On this point they further referred to the provisions contained in Section 299 PPC. Learned SPP Muhammad Asghar Rokary has conceded on this preposition but learned SPP Burhan Moazzam Malik has put his strong objection on this preposition and vehemently argued that all the three accused are major as they have attained the age of puberty. He has referred to the statement of PW-11 Dr. Imtiaz Bhatti categorically opined about the age of two accused namely Shahzad and Nadeem as per his report, both the above mentioned accused have attained the age of puberty and in a position to ejaculate. He also argued that learned defense counsel while cross-examining PW suggested that the clothes of Shahzad and Nadeem which were found stained with semen as per report of the chemical examiner were the result of their ejaculation, therefore, none of the accused can be termed as minor and their case does not fall within the provisions of Section 305 PPC. He relied upon the esteem judgements, PLD 1965 Supreme Court 363, PLD 191 S.C 172 and 179, 1991 P.Cr.L.J 928, 1997 P Cr.L.J 1150. I have gone through the esteemed judgments referred above.

"The criterion to differentiate between the minor and major is the definition as per age: either a child has attained the age of puberty or is of 18 years but this definition is available in Hadood [Islamic Law] cases and in Section 299 PPC, the definition of minor a person who is not an adult and in the present case the prosecution had to get examined the accused through Oxcitication test for the determination of their age but has failed to discharge this liability, therefore, by giving the benefit of doubt which is the right of the accused consider Sabir and Nadeem accused as minor but I am of confirmed view that Shahzad alias Sajid alias Guddu accused is more than 18 years of age and is an adult person.

Now I would like to discuss some important aspect of the demeanor of principal accused Javed Iqbal Mughal. He is a married man having two wives and two children but is living separated for more than 16 years and since then he had not seen even his own children. During the course of proceedings of the case he has been changing his attitude and many a time he had tried to deceive the Court by advancing different stories and versions. He is a Satan in the shape of a human being. In fact he is a beast and such a cruel man that it is disgrace of the humanity to label him as human. Javed Iqbal accused during the proceeding in reply to the query of this court admitted before me that he involved some innocent persons in the instant case by writing their names in the diaries because he had the grudge against them on one pretext or the other and even the name of his real brother is mentioned in the said diaries. He also stated that DIG, Lahore, Pervez Qandhari SP and Tariq Camboh DSP treated him very gently and there was no malafide on their part when they do not arrest Javed Iqbal because as per the version of Javed Iqbal he played such a successful drama before them that he is innocent and a psychiatric case. All the above said discussed evidence except extra judicial confession and judicial confession is all of circumstantial in nature and I seek the guidance from the esteemed judgement of the august Court:

"PLD 1958 Supreme Court (Pak.) 290 Allah Ditta Vs the State in which their Lordships held that where all evidence is circumstantial it is necessary that cumulatively its effect should be to exclude any reasonable hypothesis of the innocence of the accused. It was further held that by hinting at a bare possibility, no such doubt can be thought to be created as might amount to reasonable doubt within the contemplation of the criminal jurisprudence. In other words, where the chain of circumstances established against the accused person raises a strong probability that he is guilty of the offence charged, thus constituting a strong case which may be placed before a jury (in a jury trial) it is not sufficient for the accused to suggest a mere hypothesis or a remote possibility, in order to rebut that case. In order to gain a favourable verdict, it will be necessary for the accused to set up facts upon which he may rely as exculpatory circumstances [e.g. to provide an alibi] sufficient to cast a reasonable doubt over the prosecution case.

"In view of the discussion recorded above, the prosecution has fully succeeded in providing and with the grace of God I am fully convinced that the accused have committed the Qatal Amad [First Degree

Murder] of one hundred children and after cutting their dead bodies into pieces have put the dead bodies into drums recovered from the house of Javed Iqbal accused. The said drums contained the acid already discussed in this case (Formula is not recorded in the judgement for the general safety of the society) and they caused disappearance in the dead body in furtherance of their common intention. As it has been proved that the accused Javed Iqbal had more volunteer confession before the Judicial Magistrate on 13.01.2000. The case against him under Section 302, 201/34 PPC has also been proved from the other circumstantial evidence. Therefore, he is convicted and sentenced under Section 302-A PC as Qisas in 100 count. He should be strangulated through the iron chain weapon of offence in this case in the presence of legal heirs of the deceased and then his body should be cut into one hundred pieces as it has been proved that he used to cut the dead bodies of the children deceased in this case. The pieces of his dead body should be put into drum containing the formula modus operandi used by the accused for dissolving the dead bodies. Accused Javed Iqbal is also convicted under section 201 PPC in 100 count, seven years each R.I. total 700 years R.I.

"The prosecution has also succeeded in proving its case against the accused Shahzad alias Sajid alias Guddu under section 302-A PPC for committing the Qatal Amad of ninety-eight children along with the other co-accused in furtherance of their common intention. The prosecution has succeeded in proving their case through confessional statement of the accused and the circumstantial evidence. The accused should be strangulated through the weapon of offence of this case i.e. iron chain. His body should be cut into 98 pieces like the principal accused and the same should be put in the drum as recorded above. The accused is also convicted under Section 201 PCC in 98 count, seven years each total six hundred and eighty-six years R.I.

"Similarly the prosecution has succeeded in proving its case against Nadeem alias Deemi accused for committing the offence of Qatal Amad intention. It has been held that he is a minor, therefore, he is convicted under section 308 PCC as the Qisas [reparation payment] is not forcible with regard to his case. He is sentenced to fourteen years on thirteen counts, total one hundred and eighty-two years. He is also convicted under section 201 PCC on thirteen counts for causing disappearance of the dead bodies of the deceased, seven years each total ninety-one years. He is further sentenced to pay Diyat [fine] at the rate of Rs 253,625 in each count to the legal heirs of 13 deceased in favour of the State.

"Similarly the prosecution has succeeded in proving its case against the accused Sabir for committing the Qatal Amad of three children in furtherance of their common intention along with his co-accused. He is a minor and Qisas is not enforceable. Therefore, he is convicted and sentenced under Section 308 PPC fourteen years on each count, total forty-two years. He is also convicted and sentenced under Section 201 PPC for causing the disappearance of the dead bodies of the deceased in three count, total twenty-one years. He is also sentenced to pay Diyat of Rs 253,625 to the legal heirs of the deceased if the same are not available/traceable the same should be deposited in favour of State.

"The prosecution has failed to prove its case against all the accused with regard to the offences under Section 12/7/79 Hadood Ordinance and 377, 364 PCC as there is no circumstantial cooperative evidence on the record in support of the confessional statement of the accused.

"Therefore, all the accused are acquitted of the charge under Section 12/7/79 Hadood Ordinance and 364, 377 PCC.

"All the sentences will be subject to the confirmation by the Hon'ble Lahore High Court, Lahore, and will run consecutively and not concurrently. One copy of this judgment has been provided to all the accused each and they have been informed that they can file an appeal before the Hon'ble Lahore High Court, Lahore within seven days. The case property will be kept in safe custody till the result of reference/appeal/revision, if any.

Before parting with the judgement I will recommend to the

Government through the Hon'ble Lahore High Court, Lahore, that the execution of the sentence to Javed Iqbal accused and Shahzad alias Sahid alias Guddu be executed at open place preferably Minar-e-Pakistan, in the presence of the legal heirs of the deceased children in order to make it a horrible example. I would also like to appreciate the efforts made by the Special Public Prosecutor Mr. Burhan Moazzam Malik, Mr. Muhammad Ashraf Tahir, APP, Mr.Khan Abdul Wahab Khan, Counsel for the complainant, Mr. Muhammad Asghar Khan Rokari, Special Public Prosecutor, Major (R.) Aftab Ahmad and Mr. Amjad Ali Chattha as Special Public Prosecutors appointed by the Court and Mr. Najeeb Faisal, learned Defence Counsel for the principal accused, Mr. Abdul Baqi, learned Defence Counsel for Shahzad alias Sajid alias Guddu accused, Mr. Muhammad Safdar Chaudhry, learned Defence Counsel for Sabir accused and Mr. Asghar Ali Gill, learned Defence Counsel for Nadeem accused who have assisted the Court properly, spared their time especially for this case ignoring their professional engagements in order to enable this Court to decide this case within the shortest possible time as directed by Mian Muhammad Jahangir, learned District and Sessions Judge, Lahore for the expeditious disposal of this case.

"A copy of this judgment will be also sent to the Home Secretary, Government of Punjab, Lahore and Inspector General of Police, Punjab with the remarks that this Court has observed that principal accused Javed Iqbal has repeatedly mentioned the name of Ishaq alias Billa deceased, Nasim Murshad, Zafar, Yasin, Abdul Shakoor, Sub-Inspector, Abdul Khaliq, Inspector and Karamat Ali, Inspector as his co-accused with regard to the motive and commission of offence, even this Court has observed that at the time of announcement of the verdict immediately Javed Iqbal accused re-acted with the words in the presence of so many lawyers, representatives of national and international media and addressed to the Court that what decision has been made about my remaining co-accused who have not been challaned [charged]."

Sd/-(ALLAH BAKHASH RANJHA)
Additional Sessions Judge, Lahore.

⌛ 24 Interview with Anne Aguirre

Anne Aguirre and I have had numerous passionate discussions about different aspects of Javed Iqbal's story. The areas that intrigued her the most were the spiritual experiences, especially of Javed Iqbal Mughal and the subject of capital punishment from which the following interview ensued.

Anne: Looking back now, what do you think was the principle reason that inspired you to fly to Pakistan last year?

Sohail: I followed my intuition and I am glad I did that. The trip was full of surprises but it was worth it. Life offered me more than I expected. It was a mysterious and creative journey. After the trip, writing the book was also a very unusual experience for me, as I have never written a book before in which the literary and the psychiatric, the personal and the professional parts of me came together. While researching different aspects of Javed Iqbal's story I was enlightened to discover how the personal, social, religious and political lives of people are intertwined together. I feel the book will provide Western readers a few glimpses in the lives of people living in the East. In spite of living in the same decade, we live worlds apart.

Anne: For me as a Westerner, one of the most fascinating pieces of the puzzle is the saint's identification of the child Javed Iqbal as spiritually gifted. What do you make of Javed Iqbal's spiritual experiences as a child?

Sohail: I think to understand Javed Iqbal's spiritual experiences, one has to know the social, cultural and religious belief system of people. There are millions of people in Pakistan, as in many other religious communities and cultures, who are very superstitious. They believe in miracles. There are so many childless women who go to holy shrines to pray rather than consulting a medical doctor to get their infertility investigated.

I also believe that such simple, innocent and uneducated people are quite suggestible and it is easy for saints and religious gurus to hypnotize such individuals and groups. I feel that Javed Iqbal as a little boy, must have had some extraordinary qualities for the saint to choose him as a potential savior and then hypnotize him. Since the whole community consisted of his disciples, it was easy for him to declare Javed Iqbal as their local Healer, the local Messiah. I think the saint wanted to recruit Javed Iqbal for his shrine and was disappointed when his father brought him back to be set free from all those mystical experiences. It is not much different than those people in North America who visit faith healers quite frequently or those religious communities who believe in talking in tongues.

To be honest with you, there is a part of that story that is a mystery for me also. It would have been interesting to assess Javed Iqbal when he was in those trances. But then I am talking as a mental health professional, not as an expert on mysticism. Since I do not believe in religious miracles, I look for rational and scientific explanations. For people who believe in those miracles, it is a matter of faith, and they have different reactions because of their convictions. It is an area that needs in-depth exploration by psychologists who have a keen interest in spiritual experiences. William James' book, Varieties of Religious Experience and Abraham Maslow's Religions, Values and Peak Experiences are serious attempts to understand religious and spiritual experiences from the scientific and secular points of view.

I feel we have yet not reached a stage of human understanding where scientists, mystics and religious scholars agree on the nature of such spiritual experiences. It is an area where language seems very inadequate. Religious terms can be very misleading in scientific discussions. Different people in various parts of the world mean different things by the same expressions. We have yet not developed a secular vocabulary for the spiritual dimension of life. I have dealt with some of these issues in my book From Islam to Secular Humanism.

Anne: But what do you think of Javed Iqbal's relationship with God and religion as an adult?

Sohail: It is one of the biggest contradictions of Javed Iqbal's story. On one hand he fantasized about killing a hundred children and on the other hand kept on praying to God to help him in his project. I could not believe my eyes when I read the last page of his diary. After finishing his project he wrote, "We were happy that the count of one hundred was complete. We congratulated each other. I was so thankful to God for helping me complete my project that I had tears in my eyes. We celebrated all day long and ate sweets."

Anne: It is clear from your writings and your discussions of Javed Iqbal that you do not support the death sentence in his case. In the West many people who are in favor of capital punishment feel that the $50,000 per year that it costs to keep each serial killer in jail could be spent on other human welfare activities. What are your views on capital punishment?

Sohail: For me it is not an economic or financial issue, it is an ethical and moral dilemma. I do not believe we as human beings, individually or collectively, have the right to kill another human being. I think by supporting the notion of capital punishment we are essentially doing the same thing that we are criticizing. We are collectively giving permission to the judge or the jury to decide to take another human being's life. I believe that rather than killing the criminal, the goal should be to protect the community and reform and rehabilitate the criminal. Being a humanist, I believe what Eric Fromm once wrote: "Even the most sadistic and destructive man is human, as human as a saint."

I also believe that most killers are one-time killers. They killed someone in the heat of passion but they would never kill another human being again whether they live in a jail, a psychiatric hospital or the community for the rest of their lives. We need to take every step to protect society but not by taking people's lives.

Anne: And what would they be and why?

Sohail: There seem to be two groups with two distinct attitudes towards people who get involved in illegal, anti-social and immoral activities. The first group sees such people as criminals or sinners and wants to punish them. The second group tries to understand such people and has a compassionate attitude towards them. I belong to the second group.

I am also aware that a number of murderers and criminals are also creative people. If given an opportunity in jail they can write insightful books and create masterpieces, thus serving the community indirectly.

We also know that a number of people who were executed were proven innocent after the fact, but then it was too late to make amends. To kill innocent people because of insufficient evidence or hasty decisions is one of the most unfortunate situations in any community.

I am also concerned about the judicial system accepting confessions at face value. In North America in the recent past, a number of people have made false confessions in order to achieve the status of being declared a notorious serial killer. They all wanted to be celebrities. Peter Worthington, a Canadian journalist, wrote about Clifford Olson who confessed to fifty murders, Henry Lee Lucas who confessed to more than a hundred murders, and Michael McGray who said he killed 13 people, that in a bid for the notoriety that comes with being the baddest of them all, some admissions are more about mass deception than mass murder.

In countries like Pakistan, where police officers and their investigation cannot be trusted, it is even more difficult to determine the truth. These are some of the reasons I am against capital punishment and in favor of Therapeutic Prisons. I think it is the responsibility of politicians, lawyers and mental health professionals of every community to collaborate to devise a system that is compassionate and humanistic, rather than judgmental and punitive.

Anne: There is one last question I want to ask you. Do you find any similarities between Javed Iqbal and the judge?

Sohail: Yes, quite a few. They are both products of the same socio-cul-
         tural environment with the same unresolved conflicts, both
         motivated by anger and revenge, both fantasized about taking
         other human lives and both used God's name to rationalize
         their actions. Both hope to achieve celebrity status. They want
         to leave their names in the history books

⊠ 25 *The Day of Judgement*

It is March 16th, 2001 and I am reminiscing about the evening when I
heard the news on the television and saw the images of Javed Iqbal
and the judge Allah Bakhash Ranjha for the first time. Those images
had such an impact that they inspired me to go on a mysterious journey,
a journey that enticed me to explore the darkest corners of the human
soul.

Whenever I imagine the day when the judge gave the verdict, his
voice ringing with barely controlled anger this scenario appears in my
mind and completely blots out any other thought.

The sun was radiating fire that day. City streets deserted. Birds
were crouched, hiding in trees, dogs under bridges and children in
their mothers' laps. But there was one exception. The courtroom in the
heart of Lahore was choked wall to wall with people. They were afraid
to seek relief in the fresh air not wanting to risk losing their space, the
valuable space they had secured by arriving early in the morning long
before the court proceedings were to start. In spite of the heat and the
dust, hundreds of men and women, including the elderly, and children
held aloft had gathered from many villages across the country. Those
forced to stand outside the courtroom, covered their heads with caps
and shawls to protect from heatstroke. Never had anyone seen such a
big gathering in such a small courtroom in the history of Lahore. They
patiently awaited the verdict on Javed Iqbal, accused of abusing and
killing one hundred children.

When Javed Iqbal looked around, he saw many friends and foes,
neighbours and colleagues, and lovers and rivals anxiously waiting for

the judge to take his place at the highest seat in the room. The case was so intriguing and disturbing from legal and moral points of view that well-known lawyers and journalists, saints and sinners were present that scorching afternoon to hear the last chapter of this unbelievable saga.

Finally the judge arrived in his traditional black robe. As he entered the courtroom, a sudden silence fell, a silence that made many hearts beat faster. The judge looked around very seriously as if acknowledging each set of hundreds of eyes focused on him at that historical moment. Perhaps he wondered just who was the man of the hour, the man of honour he or the accused Javed Iqbal.

Once seated, he paused as the court became deathly, and raised his eyes to stare once again at the prisoner he began to narrate the verdict in a slow and reserved tone, "The prosecution has fully succeeded in proving and with the grace of God I am fully convinced that the accused have committed the Qatal Amad murder of one hundred children and after cutting their dead bodies into pieces have put the dead bodies into drums recovered from the house of Javed Iqbal accused. The accused has denied these allegations...."

The judge looked at the audience, again to let his words sink in, took a deep breath, stared straight ahead and intoned, "Because he is a Satan in the shape of a human being, in fact he is a beast and such a cruel man, that it is a disgrace of the humanity to label him as human. He should be strangulated through the iron chain weapon of offence in this case, in the presence of legal heirs of the deceased, and then his body should be cut in one hundred pieces as it has been proved that he used to cut the dead bodies of the children deceased in this case. The pieces of his dead body should be put into the drum containing the formula modus operandi used by the accused for dissolving the dead body ... the sentence be executed at an open place preferably Minar-e-Pakistan, in the presence of the legal heirs of the children in order to make it a horrible example."

When the judge finished talking, he looked around as if he were waiting for applause from the spectators. The silence hung over the courtroom, everyone afraid to breathe. The judge was sweating profusely as he suddenly realized that he had become the self-proclaimed hero of this drama, the avenger, and that in the heat of passion he had crossed a line where he should not have gone, declaring in his anger and disgust, things he should not have.

People in the courtroom looked extremely sad, or angry and upset but Javed Iqbal was calm, emotionless and steadfast as before. He had shackles on his feet and a rosary draped across his hand, a rosary that made others nervous, as they remembered his early childhood as a "Chosen One" with special powers.

Javed Iqbal looked around once again and found himself surrounded by hundreds of people. Would he have stood with head held high as he asked himself,

"Am I the Christ of this generation who is offered a crown of thorns?

Am I the Socrates of this century who is about to be given a cup of poison?

Am I the Mansoor of this era who is ordered to be crucified?"

He might suddenly have remembered those Quranic verses in which Moses traveled with Khizr. When Khizr killed an innocent child and Moses, shocked, asked for an explanation, Khizr said, "These are mystical matters, you would not understand them. This is a mystery that is not revealed to everyone."

Javed Iqbal was quite aware that mystics did things that priests and judges did not follow because they followed the words, not the spirit of the law and scriptures. They judged people, declared them sinners and criminals and ordered them to be hanged, stoned to death or to burn in hell. Javed Iqbal knew that he had challenged authorities, traditions and moral norms of his community and as a result he was going to be "crucified". In the depths of his heart he had accepted his fate, he was no longer afraid of death. He believed he was *The Chosen One*. That was why he looked peaceful and felt tranquil, and that peacefulness was becoming a frightening mystery for the people around him.

"They can kill me, but if the environment and circumstances do not change, there will be another Javed Iqbal."

There are no realities, only perceptions.

~ Anonymous

Epilogue

🕱   *Suicide or Murder of the Truth?*

On October 10th, 2001, my friend Zahid Ali Lodhi sent me a news-paper article stating that Javed Iqbal Mughal and his partner Sajid, had committed suicide by hanging themselves with their bed-sheets in adjacent cells in Kot Lakhpat Jail, Lahore. The Toronto Sun also reported, "A Pakistani man sentenced to be strangled, chopped into 100 pieces and dissolved in acid for the murders of dozens of children has been found dead in his cell in an apparent suicide...."

When Anne, my colleague, read the news, she enquired, "What do you think?"

"I don't believe it." I responded spontaneously.

"Why not?"

"First of all, it seems highly unlikely for two people to commit suicide at the same time in separate cells, especially by hanging. If they were in the same cell and they had acquired some poison or a gun, I might have believed such a report. But I remember being in that death cell. The ceiling was very high and there were no hooks on the walls, so I hardly think it would have been possible to hang oneself."

"Then what do you think happened?"

"I would not be surprised if they were murdered."

In the next few days, as more information became available, it was reported that the deaths took place between midnight and 2 a.m. The officer in charge did not report the deaths and left the jail under mysterious circumstances. Even the officer who relieved him did not report the deaths until the bodies were discovered in the morning. It seemed very suspicious.

According to the post mortem reports, there was no evidence of hanging. "The initial autopsy findings of the mass murderer Javed Iqbal and his accomplice Sajid, who were found dead in their death cells in

Kot Lakhpat Jail on Tuesday, indicate that both died of strangulation while they also got their necks broken...The sources said that strangulation could only be the cause of death of both".

The deaths of Javed Iqbal and Sajid sound very much like that of Ishaq Billa. An investigation has been ordered of the conduct of the Chief Warden of the Jail and the officers in charge, reminiscent of that of the police officers of Qilla Gujar Singh, who were charged with the murder of Ishaq Billa.

It was interesting to note that Javed Iqbal's case was recently forwarded from the High Court to the Federal Shariat [Islamic] Court because of its unique nature. Javed Iqbal's lawyer, Faisal Najib, in his interview with the newspaper Nation, stated that "...the government was aware of the fact that it was a case of no evidence and there were maximum chances of the acquittal of the appellant." He maintained that jail officials probably followed the directions of some high-ups in the government, who had decided to close this chapter forever by killing Javed Iqbal.

It was also significant that Javed Iqbal had recently sent an application to the Lahore High Court in which he claimed that "... jail officials had been putting blades and other sharp materials in his cell prompting him to commit suicide. Mughal claimed that he had not killed 100 children, but they were all alive and protected at a hidden place only known to him. He had also said that he would disclose the ' hidden place', if he was provided an opportunity to address a Press conference or allowed to appear before the honorable court". Javed Iqbal repeatedly accused the authorities by stating, " They are afraid of me and do not want me to disclose the 'truth'."

The family of Javed Iqbal refused to accept the dead body. Ironically, I received so many emails and phone calls from all over the world about his death, that I felt that apart from his state-appointed lawyer, I was the only human being in the whole wide world who cared what happened to that man who had struggled with his inner and outer demons.

Javed Iqbal's death is as surrealistic as his life. He was so extraordinary all his life that he could not simply die an ordinary death. Even after his death the mystery continues. A number of Pakistani newspapers have reported that the police officers who guard the grave have reported seeing dangerous snakes crawling out of his grave at night. The snakes mysteriously disappear when the police try to kill them. I wonder whether those hallucinatory venomous snakes are more a reflection of Javed Iqbal's grandiose dreams of fame, or of the nightmare of the correctional and justice systems of a nation who loves superstitions more than realities.

Did Javed Iqbal commit suicide or was he murdered?

The mystery continues, and will continue to expand and grow for years, decades, even centuries, because it is being created from *The Myth of The Chosen One.*

October 28th, 2001.
Whitby, Canada

Dr. K. Sohail

Pervez Iqbal, Dr. Sohail, Waseem Iqbal, Saeed Iqbal.

Abid Hasan Minto (Senior Advocate Supreme Court of Pakistan) being interviewed by Dr. Sohail.

Kot Lakhpat Jail, Lahore.

Dr. Sohail outside Kot Lakhpat Jail, Javed Iqbal's prision.

D r . K . S o h a i l

Minar-e-Pakistan (Tower of Pakistan) where Javed Iqbal was sentenced to be publicly hanged.

The Myth of the Chosen One

Javed Iqbal in newspaper office "confessing" to journalists.

Javed Iqbal in court with his co-accused young partners.

One of the barrels said to be used for dissolving human remains.

The Myth of the Chosen One   185

Judge Allah Bakhash Ranjha

The shoes of 100 missing children.

D r . K . S o h a i l

Javed Iqbal adding his signature to the verdict declaring him guilty.

About the Author

Dr. Khalid Sohail's most recent book, FROM ISLAM TO SECULAR HUMANISIM, was released in the summer of 2001. He is also published as a poet, short story anthologist, philosopher, and anthologies contributor. He is a documentary film producer, owner of Darvesh Films (Canada), lecturer, and has appeared many times on broadcast media. Dr. Sohail enjoys a successful practice as a psychotherapist at his Creative Psychotherapy Clinic in Whitby, Ontario, Canada, where he has combined many new techniques with his love of people to assist with the healing of his patients.

"Just call me Sohail" he'll say upon meeting, his open, unpretentious smile radiating a warmth that makes you immediately realize the great humanitarian values that are the underpinnings of his life. Even after a brief social encounter you'll feel better knowing him, and how important you are as an individual, an equal, irrespective of your background.

This book is part of Sohail's continuing journey seeking knowledge for himself to help others, and justice and fairness for all. Dr. Sohail's writing is an adjunct to his practice as one of Canada's leading psychiatric healers. Publications by Dr. Sohail are many and varied.

BOOKS

Pages Of My Heart (Poems)
Mother Earth Is Sad (Stories)
Literary Encounters (Interviews)
Mixed Marriages (Sociology)
From One Culture To Another (Psychotherapy with Immigrants)
Strangers Care (Group Psychotherapy)
Schizophrenia...Accepting a Challange (Psychotherapy)
Encounters With Depression (Psychotherapy)
Growing Alone—Growing Together (Marital Therapy)
Books are available on CD

Video Documentaries

Intimate Encounters (Mixed Marriages)
Mixed Messages (Children of Mixed Marriages)
Encounters With Depression
Growing Alone...Growing Together (Marital Problems)
Breaking The Cycle (Encounters With Domestic Violence)

Available at www.creativepsychotherapy.com

Message from the Publisher

Death is always and under all circumstances a tragedy, for if
it is not, then it means that life has become one.
— Theodore Roosevelt, March 12, 1900.

When informed of the topic of my second editing project with Dr. Sohail, I had to shut off the horror that was flooding the creative side of my mind and let myself rely strictly on logic.

I sat listening, almost without comment or question, to my learned colleague until he finished explaining why he had written such a horrific documentary.

Upon discovery of a court's verdict while watching TV, and by what may appear to be instinct alone, he had rushed half-way around the world to interview the man alleged to have abused and murdered one hundred children, who claimed to be seeking revenge for the death of his mother!

Throughout Sohail's commentary the nagging question continued, "Was I ready to accept the responsibility of helping to develop and publish such a revelation?"

After serious contemplation over the next few days, I knew that it was a story needing to be told. But if it had not been for the close association with the Crime Writers of Canada, I would have had a much more difficult time with the topic.

What is especially intriguing about this work is the wondering if the accused committed the horrible crimes or not. Like all our books, we would be interested in your comments.

V. Wm. (Bill) Belfontaine
Publisher
Email: whitekn@istar.ca